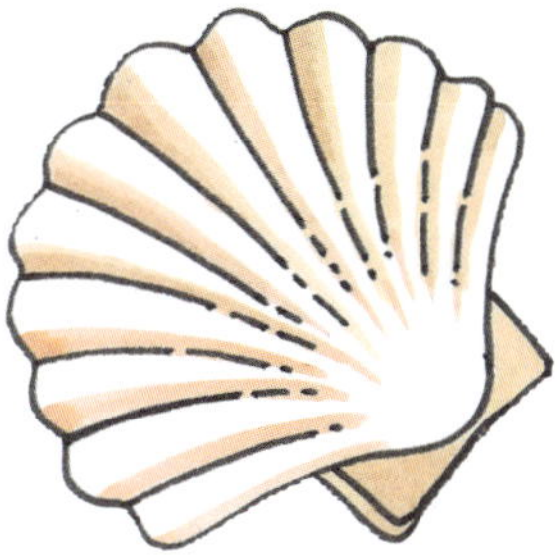

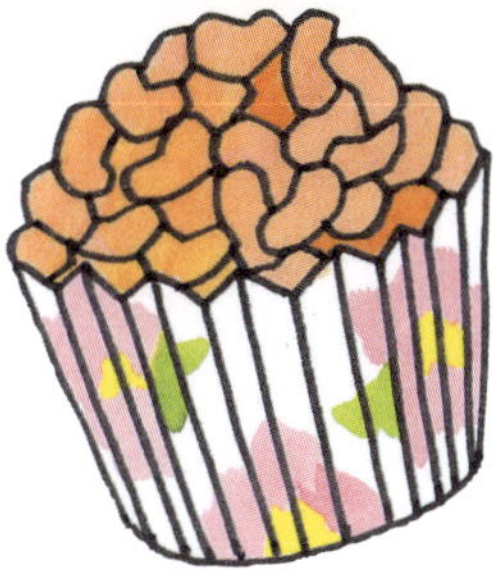

My Big Book of SUMMER Activities

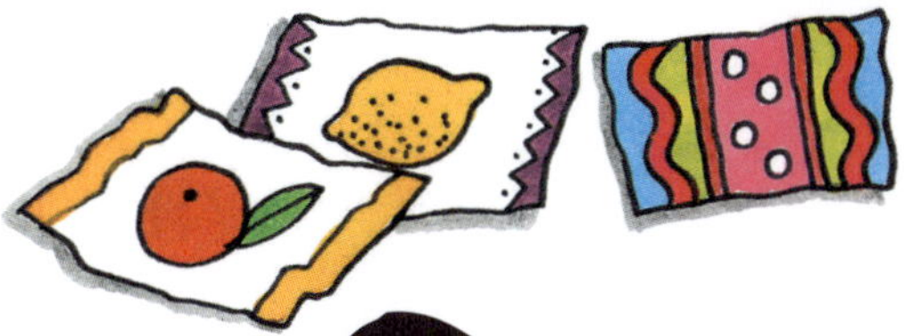

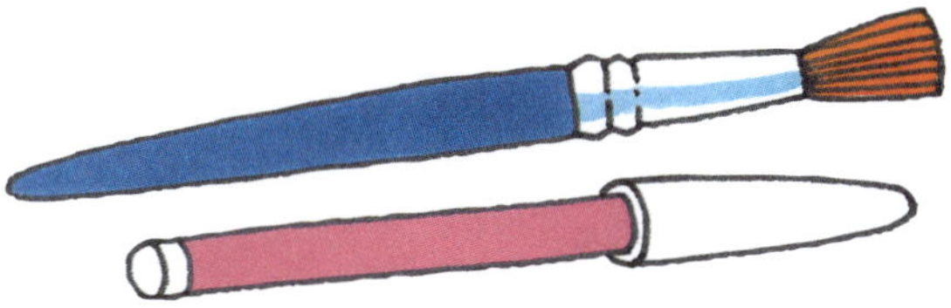

PACKED WITH CREATIVE CRAFTS TO MAKE
AND OUTDOOR ACTIVITIES TO DO

Written and illustrated by

Clare Beaton

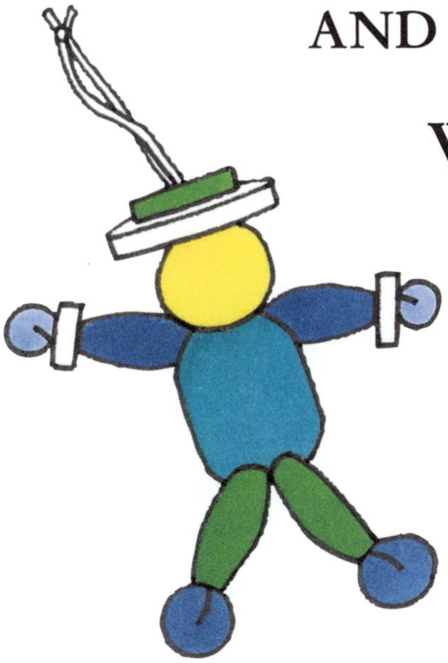

Contents

Turn off the TV   page 3
Switch off the TV and be creative!
Crafts, games, and activities, many with a TV theme.

Fun with Friends   page 27
Stuck for something to do with your friends?
Pages of great, creative ideas.

Fresh Air Fun   page 51
Time to go out into the garden, park, or countryside.
Lots of activities to inspire you.

Travel Fun   page 75
Off on a trip—by car, train, boat, or plane?
Loads of great ideas to make the trip fly past.

More card games
(See also pages 41 and 82.)

Pelmanism (pairs game)

For two or three players

The idea of the game is to collect as many pairs as possible. Place the cards face down on a flat surface. The first player turns over two cards so everyone can see them and, if they are a pair, picks them up. A pair is the same rank and color, so a 6 of hearts and a 6 of diamonds (both red) or a Queen of spades and a Queen of clubs (both black). If not, turn them face down again in exactly the same place. The next player then turns over two cards, and so on, until all the cards are paired up. The winner is the one with the most pairs.

The trick is to try and remember what and where all the cards are! (Sometimes this game is called "Concentration.")

Snap

For two or more players

Deal out all the cards, face down. In turns, each place a card face up on a pile in the middle (do *not* peek first). When a card matches the last card on the pile, everyone shouts SNAP! as quickly as they can. The first person to shout gets the whole pile and starts a new pile. Carry on, in turns. The game ends when one player wins all the cards. (This can be a noisy game so it's best not to play it in a crowded plane or train!)

 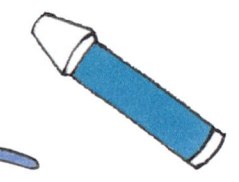

Before you begin

There is nothing wrong with watching TV, but don't let it take over your life. There are so many other great things you can get up to in your free time. Switch off for a while and have some fun with this book. Some of the ideas in next few pages are TV-linked. You can even do some of them in front of the TV, if you really can't miss your favorite programs!

Some basic tools and materials:
paint and brushes
varnish
glue
scissors and craft knife
paper and card stock
colored pencils and felt-tip pens

 **This symbol is to remind you to take care when you use a craft knife.**

- Always take great care with sharp tools such as scissors, needles, and knives.
- Always cover work surfaces with newspaper before you start to paint or varnish your work.
- When using a craft knife always cut away from hands. Use thick card stock or something similar under whatever you are cutting. Cut slowly and lightly several times.
- Wash your hands and wear an apron before preparing food.
- You can find most of the materials used in this book, like cardboard boxes, for free, or you will already have them at home. Recycle wire coat-hangers, old buttons, newspapers, and foil food containers.

This sweet will be hiding on pages 6 to 26. See if you can spot it each time.

How to trace from templates

1. Trace the template shape using tracing paper, masking tape, and a pencil.
2. Turn over the tracing paper and scribble over the lines with a soft pencil.
3. Turn over and tape on to paper or card stock. Retrace over the lines firmly.

Initials and logos

Your **initials** are the first letters of your first and last names.
So Mary Smith's initials are MS and John Brown's are JB.

Artists sometimes use their initials instead of their whole name when they are signing their pictures or sculpture. The famous French painter called Toulouse Lautrec signed his work like this:

Albrecht Dürer, a German artist who lived over 400 years ago, signed his work like this:

Try making a pattern with your initials. You can join the letters together. You can make one smaller than the other, or you can overlap them.

Years ago, rich people would have their initials everywhere, on their silver cutlery, embroidered on their clothes and handkerchiefs, stamped on their luggage, and painted on their plates.

Grow your initials in cress. Sprinkle the seeds on a damp paper towel.

Lightly pencil the letters on the paper towel as a guide.

Companies use special symbols called **logos** to look attractive and so we remember them. They are used everywhere from company stationery and ads, to trucks and airplanes. The best are usually simple ones.

Television companies also have them. Try "logo spotting" when you are watching TV or when you are out and about. You could keep a collection in a notebook.

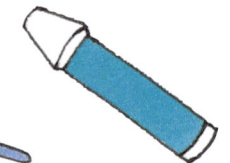

Plastic TV stars

What you will need
- ★ TV magazines
- ★ scissors
- ★ clear PVC folder (thick or thin)
- ★ clean dish towel
- ★ iron
- ★ hole punch
- ★ needle and thread
- ★ double-sided tape
- ★ darning needle and yarn

Warning!
Only use an iron with the thick PVC. Don't use an iron on your own. Ask a grown-up to help or supervise.

TIP
Remember when you are arranging your words and pictures, that BOTH sides will be seen. So you need to place the first bits face down and the next face upwards.

1
Cut or tear out pictures and words from magazines.

2
Cut folder into pieces. Take one piece and separate it into two.

3
Arrange your pictures between the two pieces of plastic, like a "sandwich" (see TIP).

Thick folders only
Put a dish towel on the ironing board. Put the plastic "sandwich" on it and fold the towel over it.

Using a hot iron, slowly move it back and forth, pressing down, for about 2 minutes.

Trim around the plastic if you want a different shape.
Leave the "sandwich" to cool. Turn the iron off. Punch a hole in the plastic.

Here are three alternative ways of joining together THIN PVC.

Tape shouldn't be all covered by pictures.

Cover bottom folder piece in double-sided tape. Stick down picture and cover with other PVC piece carefully.

Make a plastic picture sandwich. With needle and thread sew around edge.

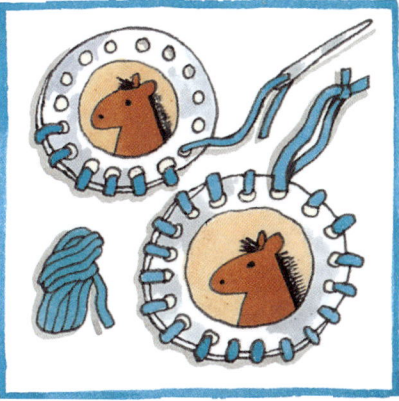

Using a hole punch, make holes around shape. Over-sew with colored yarn.

Labels and decorations

Cut out in different shapes and hang from rucksacks, school bags, buttons, or drawer knobs.

Bookmarks

Add a tassel.

MORE IDEAS
★ Thread thin ribbon, cord, plastic string, or raffia through holes.
★ Cut out in pinking shears.
★ Scatter glitter or sequins around the pictures before you sandwich them.
★ For a bag label, put your name and address on one side.

Key-ring

Use a metal ring to make a key-ring.

Small book

Punch two holes on one side of the "pages" and tie together.

Safety-pin jewelery

This jewelery is very special. No one would ever guess that the main component is ordinary safety-pins! **Be patient!** It takes time but it looks fabulous.

small glass beads of all colors

different sizes and shapes of plastic or glass beads

different-sized safety-pins

thin cord elastic

thin colored cord

Brooch

Warning! Take care with the open safety-pins.

What you will need
★ 1 large safety-pin, several small ones
★ large different-colored beads

1

Open the smaller safety-pins and thread on the beads. Close them.

2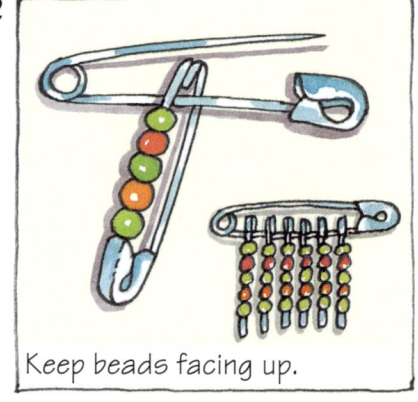

Keep beads facing up.

Open the large pin. Thread the beaded pins over end with the closed end at top.

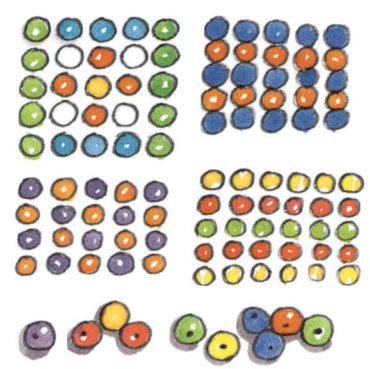

By threading beads on in different orders, you can make all sorts of patterns.

Sparkling bracelet

What you will need
★ 80 safety-pins about 1 in long
★ 240 small colored beads
★ 2 x 12-in. lengths of thin elastic

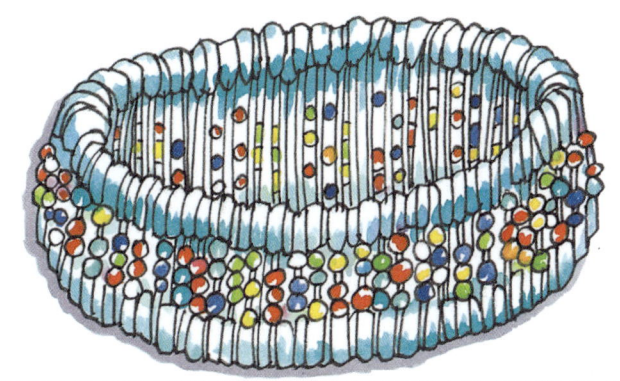

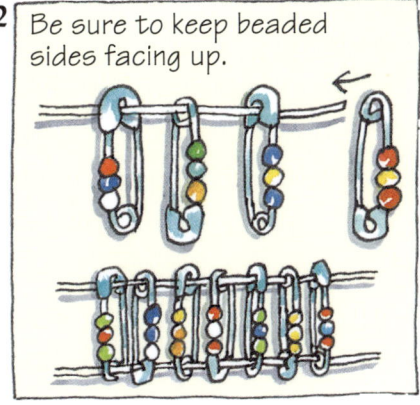

Open each safety-pin and thread on three beads. Use one color, two colors, or mixed colors.

Thread the safety-pins on to one piece of elastic, alternately top and bottom, then thread the second piece through.

When all the safety-pins are threaded, knot the ends together twice on the wrong side. Cut the ends.

Necklace

What you will need
★ different-sized safety-pins
★ colored beads
★ 30-in. length of colored cord

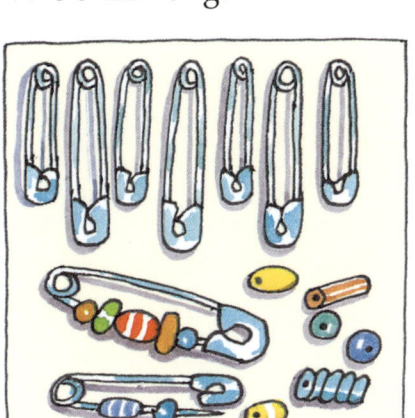

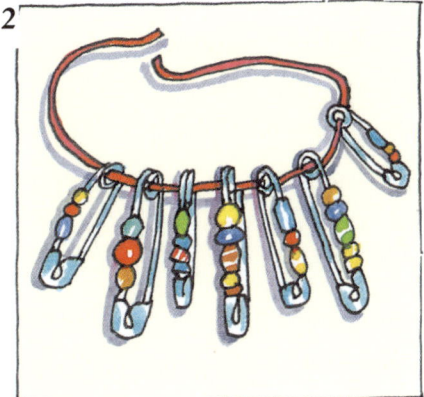

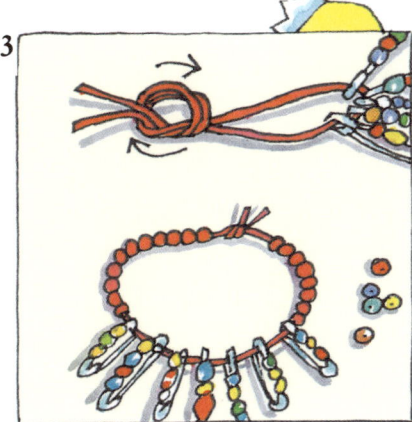

Arrange the safety-pins with closed ends together and thread on the beads.

Thread the safety-pins on to the cord with the beads facing up.

Knot the ends of the cord and slip over head. Or thread more beads either side of the pins before knotting.

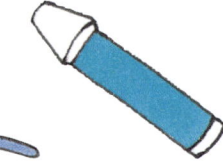

Door sign

Make a sign to hang from your door knob. Decorate it and write a message on either side.

What you will need
★ thin card stock or stiff paper
★ pencil and tracing paper
★ colored pens or pencils
★ scissors

1 Using the template below and the instructions on page 4, draw the outline on to the card or paper.

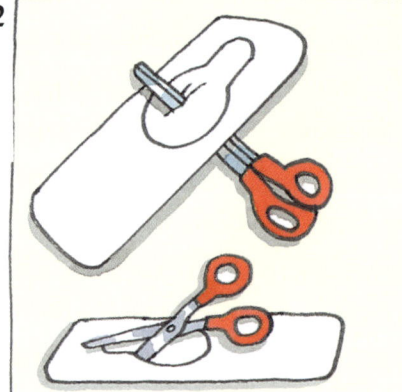

2 Cut out. Push the end of closed scissors into the hole and then cut out the hole.

3 Decorate and write a message or your name on both sides of the sign. Hang on your door.

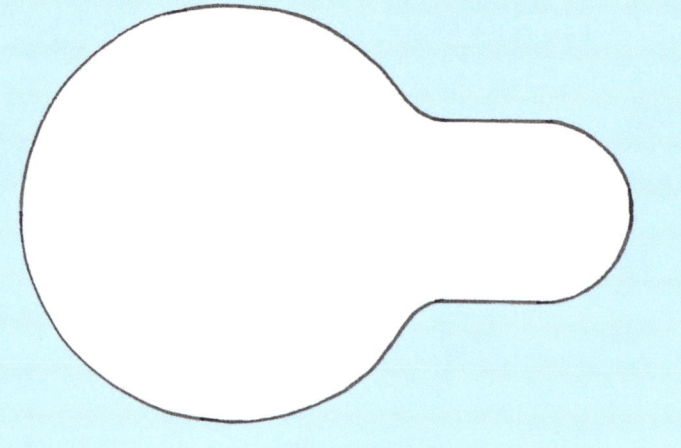

Make a door sign for a friend or relative as a present.

Ice cream sodas

A delicious cooling drink to enjoy on a hot day, or even in front of the TV with your friends! This is really simple to make.

What you will need
- ★ vanilla ice cream
- ★ tall glass and straw
- ★ soda or sparkling lemonade

1
Put a scoop of ice cream into a tall glass.

2
Fill up the glass with soda or lemonade.

3
Drink with a straw!

Paper slippers

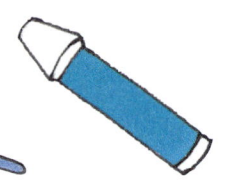

What you will need
- ★ large newspapers
- ★ PVA glue
- ★ sticky tape
- ★ paint and brush
- ★ other decorations, like stickers or glitter

1 Making the sole

Open a sheet of newspaper and fold it in two, lengthways. Fold it up into a long strip about 1.5 in. wide.

2

Fold over 3 in. of the end of the paper strip. Glue down. Now keep winding the strip around, gluing as you go.

3

Add on more paper strips, winding around tightly and pressing together to make a firm block.

4

Keep adding glued strips until the length of the shoe's sole is a little longer than your foot.

5 Making the strap

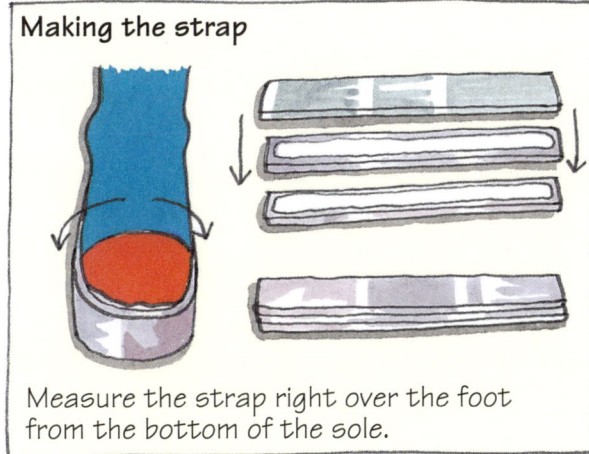

Measure the strap right over the foot from the bottom of the sole.

6

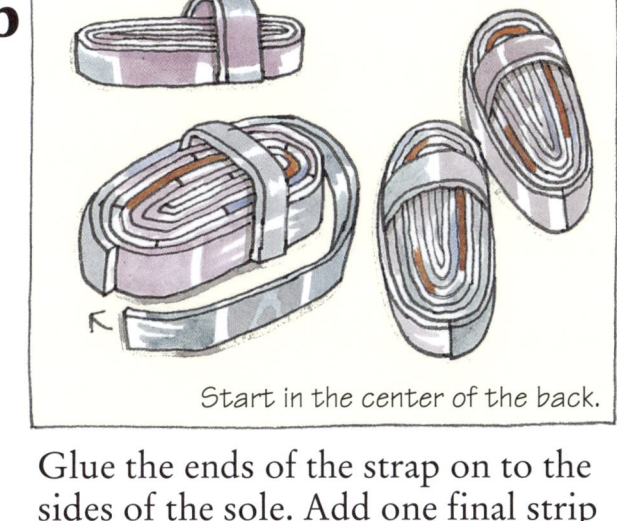

Start in the center of the back.

Measure the length needed. Glue three paper strips of the right length together.

You can now decorate your slippers in any way you like.

Paint
If you paint them, put the paint on very thickly and only paint the straps and the side of the sole.

Glue the ends of the strap on to the sides of the sole. Add one final strip to finish the sole and cover the strap.

Collage
Tear or cut out pictures from comics or magazines. Glue them on.

Fabric bow
Glue fabric around the side of the sole. Cut two strips of fabric the same width but double the length of the strap. Glue them on the straps, starting at the sides. Tie the loose ends together on top in a bow.

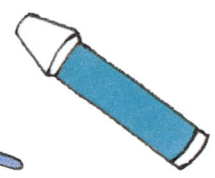

Button and bead people

These button and bead figures can be made from wooden and plastic beads of all shapes and sizes. You can use pearl, colored, and plastic buttons too. They make great gifts for your friends or your teacher.

Button person

What you will need
★ buttons
★ round bead for the head
★ 4 buttons for the hands and feet
★ 2 x 14-in. lengths strong thread

1 round bead for head

Sort the buttons into groups for the legs, arms, and body.

2 Legs — end button for foot

Fold the two lengths of thread in half. Thread buttons on as shown to make two legs.

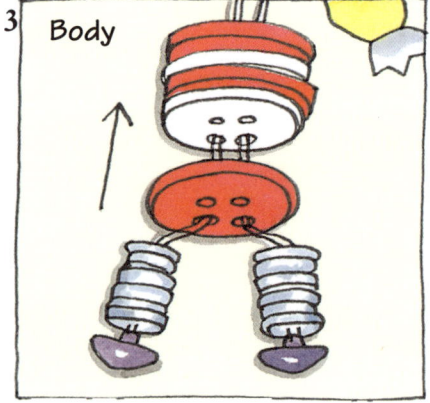

3 Body

Pull the four threads from the legs through two holes in the body buttons.

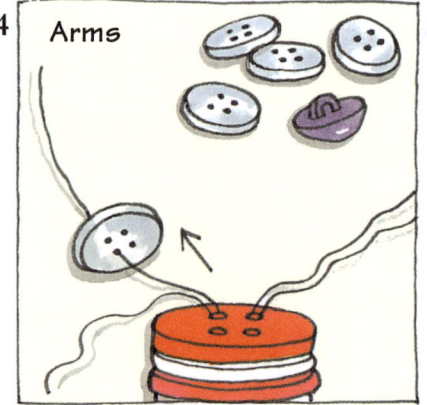

4 Arms

Separate the two pairs of thread again. Put one thread through one hole of the first arm button.

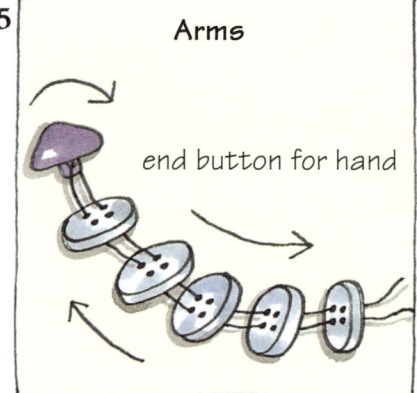

5 Arms — end button for hand

Continue threading on buttons to the end one. Then thread back through another hole.

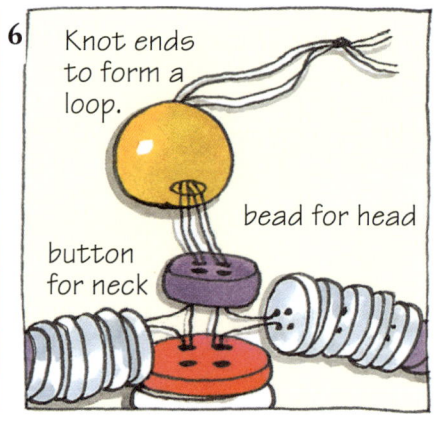

6 Knot ends to form a loop. — bead for head — button for neck

Make second arm. Put all four threads through neck button and head bead.

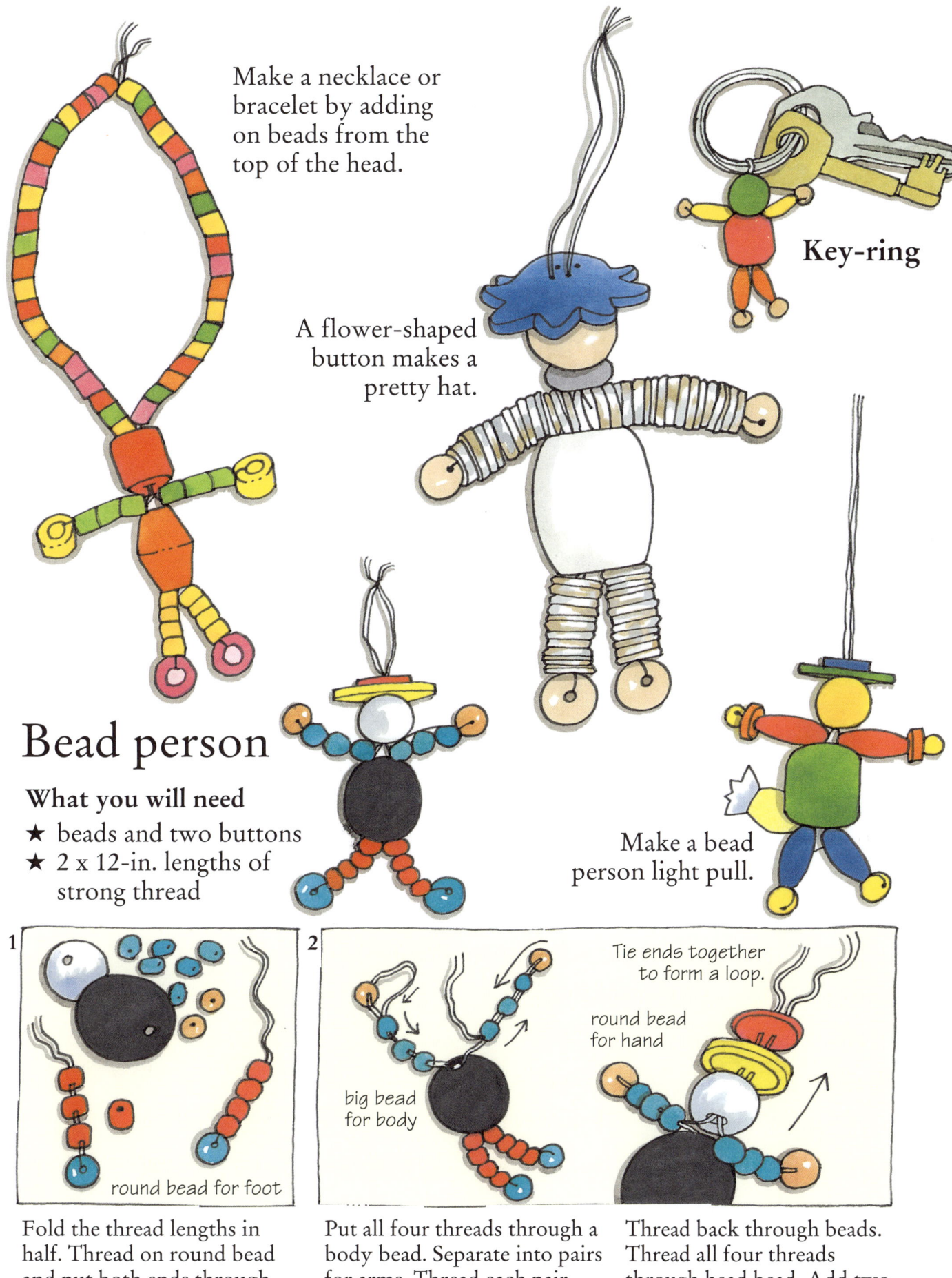

Make a necklace or bracelet by adding on beads from the top of the head.

A flower-shaped button makes a pretty hat.

Key-ring

Make a bead person light pull.

Bead person

What you will need
★ beads and two buttons
★ 2 x 12-in. lengths of strong thread

1 round bead for foot

2 big bead for body

Tie ends together to form a loop.

round bead for hand

Fold the thread lengths in half. Thread on round bead and put both ends through leg beads. Make two.

Put all four threads through a body bead. Separate into pairs for arms. Thread each pair through arm beads up to round "hands."

Thread back through beads. Thread all four threads through head bead. Add two buttons for hat.

Spot the difference

Can you spot 10 differences between these two pictures?

Fancy foil mobile

This mobile is made using a technique called *repoussé.* You press a design into metal so that it stands out in relief.

What you will need
- ★ metal foil, like fast-food containers
- ★ pencil and old ball-point pen
- ★ scissors
- ★ newspaper
- ★ wood, raffia, or string
- ★ metal coat-hanger

Warning!
Take care because foil can be sharp.

Make different shapes or vary the patterns on the same shapes, like birds or fish.

1

Draw and cut out the shape from metal foil.

2 Press down firmly—remember, you can't correct mistakes!

Place the shape on folded newspaper and draw on the design with a ball-point pen.

3 Make more and tie on to the hanger.

Make a hole at the top of the shape. Thread through yarn, raffia, or string and tie a loop.

TV snacks

Take a break from TV to make these snacks to nibble in front of your favorite programs later. Make the delicious drink on page 11 to go with them.

Egg carton nibbles

What you will need
- ★ egg carton
- ★ scissors
- ★ selection of nibbles

Cut off the lid and any flaps on the box. Fill the compartments with different nibbles.

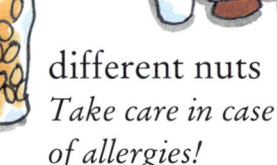

different nuts
Take care in case of allergies!

segments of orange or tangerine

small regular or cheese crackers

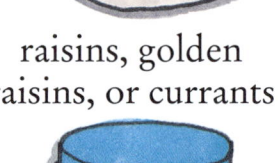

raisins, golden raisins, or currants

grapes or cherries

carrot, celery, and cucumber sticks

Marshmallow crispies

Here is a really sticky snack for a special treat. Don't forget to clean your teeth afterwards!

What you will need
- ★ 1/4 cup powdered sugar
- ★ 1/4 cup margarine
- ★ 4 tbsp corn syrup
- ★ 1 cup marshmallows
- ★ 1 cup rice crispies

Makes 18 crispies.

- heavy-based saucepan
- wooden spoon
- mixing bowl
- 18 paper cases

Warning! Ask a grown-up to help with the heating.

1

Stir occasionally.

Put the sugar, margarine, and syrup into the saucepan and heat gently until dissolved.

2

Add the marshmallows and stir until dissolved.

3

Put the rice crispies into the mixing bowl. Pour over the mixture from the saucepan and mix well.

4

Use a smaller spoon to fill cases.

Spoon into the paper cases. Leave to set. This will take about 15–20 minutes. They will be gooey!

Cartoon cardboard creatures

These cardboard creatures are great fun and easy to make. Try some of your own using different shapes or those on the templates.

What you will need
- ★ corrugated cardboard
- ★ tracing paper
- ★ pencil
- ★ craft knife and scissors
- ★ paints and brushes

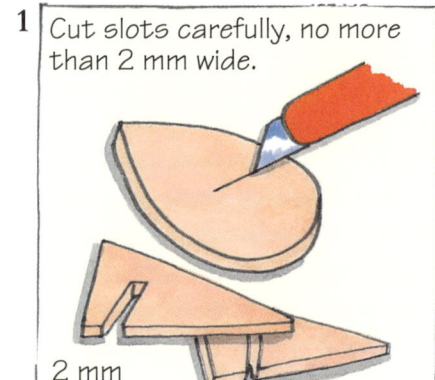

1 Cut slots carefully, no more than 2 mm wide.

2 mm

Draw and cut out the pieces from cardboard. Use the template shapes opposite and follow the instructions on page 4.

2

Paint the card. Leave to dry. Then turn over and paint the other side.

3

When dry, slot the pieces together and stand them up.

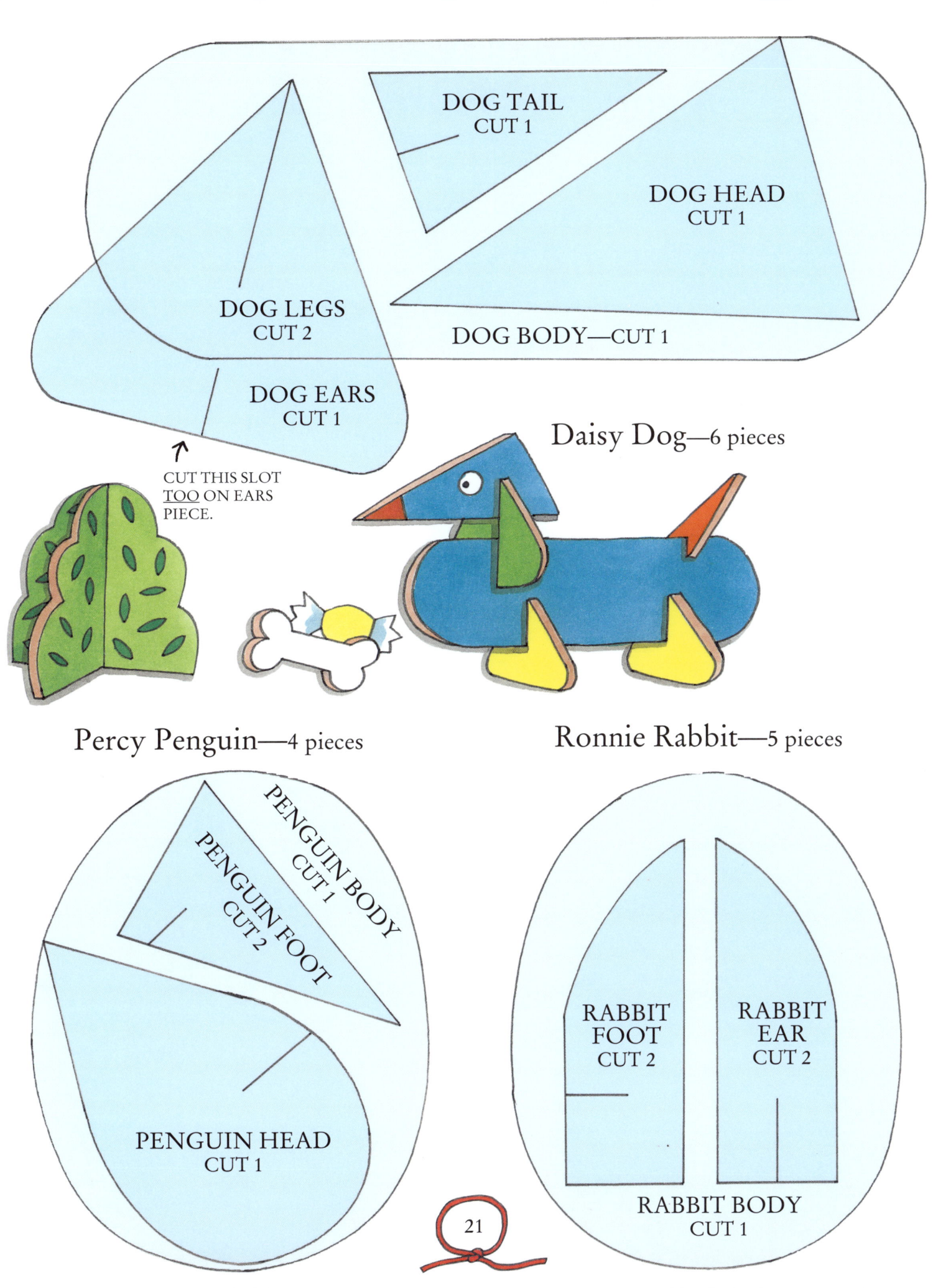

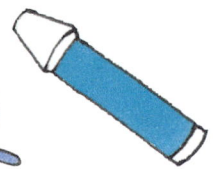

Paper and pencil games

What you will need
★ sheets of scrap paper
★ pencils

Hangman

A game for 2 players.
One player thinks of a word without telling the other player, and draws a dash for each letter.

The other player tries to guess the word by guessing a letter at a time. If the letter *is* in the word, the first player writes it in the correct position. If it *isn't,* he or she starts to draw the hanging man. The hanged man has 11 parts in all.

The winner is the player who guesses the word before the man is hanged or the other player whose word has not been guessed.

Battleships

A game for 2 players.
Each player has a fleet of ships.
1 destroyer—3 squares
1 aircraft carrier—3 squares
1 submarine—2 squares
1 patrol boat—1 square
1 frigate—2 squares

Each player draws a plan (as shown) and marks his fleet on it. Don't let the other players see! Each draws a blank plan too.

The fun is to guess the position of your opponent's boats, and sink them! You call out a grid reference, C4 or B2 and so on. So you don't make the same shot twice, mark your guesses (H for "hit" and M for "miss") on your blank plan.

Take it in turns to "fire." Make a cross on your fleet plan if your opponent hits your boat. You have to say if it is a hit or a miss. If a boat crosses several squares, all the squares have to be hit before the boat is sunk.

The winner is the one who first sinks all his opponent's fleet.

Odd one out

Look along the rows of sports pictures.
Can you spot the odd one out in each row?

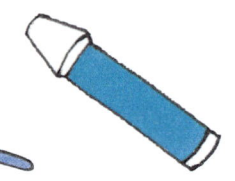

Make your own TV

Take your favorite TV program as inspiration for this mini-version. A cartoon, soap opera, cowboy, or nature program will work well.

What you will need
★ a small cardboard box
★ craft knife
★ sticky tape
★ 2 long cardboard tubes
★ ruler and pencil
★ paper and scissors
★ black paint and brush
★ felt-tip pens

1 Tape corners for strength.

Cut a hole in the bottom of the box using the craft knife. Leave a border 2 in. wide.

2 Cut out the 4 holes carefully.

Use one of the tubes to mark holes at the top and bottom of the box.

3

Cut the tubes so they are about 3 in. higher than the box.

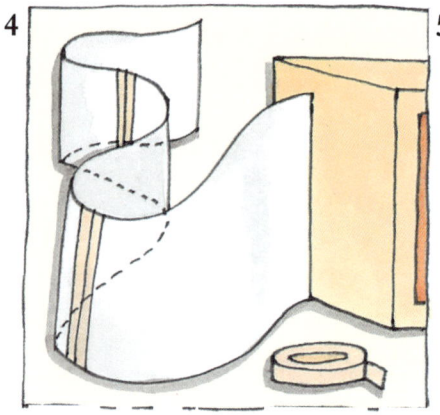

4

Cut the paper into a strip 3 in. narrower than the box depth. Tape several pieces together.

5

Paint the outside of the box with black paint. Leave to dry.

6 The story can run from right to left. Add more paper if needed.

Draw a story on the paper strip. Leave the first and last 4 in. blank. Color it in.

7 Leave some paper unrolled to fit gap.

8 Make sure the picture faces outwards.

9

Tape both ends of the strip to the center of the two tubes. Starting at the end of the story, roll the strip up on to one tube.

Push carefully into the box from the back. Fit the tubes into the holes, top and bottom.

Now turn the tubes until the start of the "film" is showing. Wind it through to the end, frame by frame.

Work out your film in "frames" before you start drawing. Give it a beginning and end. Keep it simple and make the pictures bold and colorful. You can give the commentary as you wind.

Tadpole turning into a frog. Think of other nature "stories" like this.

TV facts

Before you switch the television back on, how much do you *really* know about it?

Who invented TV and when?
A Scottish engineer, John Logie Baird, gave the first public demonstration of television on January 26th, 1926, in London. This television was made of wood and cardboard! Many engineers from other countries, like Guglielmo Marconi in Italy, Vladimir Zworykin in the USA, and Kenjiro Takayanagi in Japan, were working on the idea of television at the same time too.

How does the picture reach your TV screen?
As a television camera takes pictures of a scene the pattern of light in the pictures is made into a pattern of digital signals. Digital technology sends digital signals to your TV set. The screen is made up of thousands, sometimes even millions, of pixels. These pixels change color, switching on and off, to show you scenes from your favorite show.

What is a smart TV?
Also called a hybrid TV or a connected TV, a smart TV allows you to connect to the internet. You can stream programs on demand directly from apps as well as searching the internet or playing online games.

Did you know?
- The first president to appear on television was Franklin D. Roosevelt (FDR) in 1939 at the opening of the World Fair.

- Though television first started broadcasting in the late 1930s, the first remote control wasn't introduced until 1950, and was connected to the TV by a wire!

- People used to think that the characters on the TV could see you in your home!

Fun with Friends

Before you begin

This book is packed with friendly ideas! You can make some of them *for* your friends, like the friendship bracelets and the friendship cards. You can organize others *with* your friends, like the fundraising, the clubs, and card games. Whatever the weather and wherever you are, on vacation, at home, at school, or at your friends' houses, enjoy all the things to make and do on the following pages.

Some basic tools and materials:
paint and brushes
varnish
glue
scissors and craft knife
paper and card stock
colored pencils and felt-tip pens

 **This symbol is to remind you to take care when you use a craft knife.**

- Always take great care with sharp tools such as scissors, needles, and knives.
- Always cover work surfaces with newspaper before you start to paint or varnish your work.
- When using a craft knife always cut away from hands. Use thick card stock or something similar under whatever you are cutting. Cut slowly and lightly several times.
- Wash your hands and wear an apron before preparing food.
- You can find most of the materials used in this book, like cardboard and card stock, for free, or you will already have them at home. Recycle wire coat-hangers, old buttons, newspapers, and foil food containers.

 This ladybug will be hiding on pages 30 to 50. See if you can spot it each time.

How to trace from templates

1. Trace the template shape using tracing paper, masking tape, and a pencil.

2. Turn over the tracing paper and scribble over the lines with a soft pencil.

3. Turn over and tape on to paper or card. Retrace over the lines firmly.

Penfriends

Penfriends, or pen pals, are friends you rarely or never see, but you get to know them by writing to them.

You can write to people linked to your school or to a sports team, or to friends you meet on vacation. They might be in the same country as you or in another country.

There are organizations that arrange penfriends all over the world. Look online or ask in your local library for some more ideas.

Writing to a penfriend is like having a conversation by letter. Remember to ask questions and answer any your penfriend asks you. Exchange information about a shared interest—your favorite sport, TV show, pets, or music.

As well as news and information, you can also send newspaper or magazine cuttings, candy wrappers, photos of yourself, your family, and pets. If your penfriend lives abroad, you could collect stamps too!

Everything from a foreign country is a little different and exciting. Exchange stickers, travel and cinema tickets, for example. If your penfriend speaks another language, could you learn a few simple phrases: "hello," "goodbye," "my name is," and so on? You could record yourself and your family saying hello, along with your favorite music.

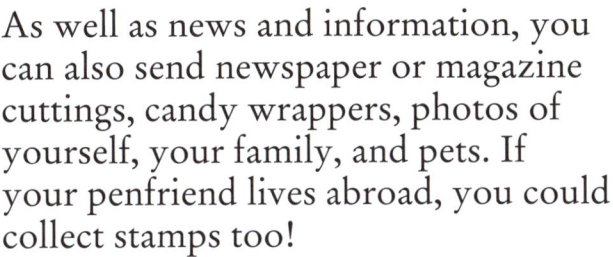

If you have access to a computer, you might be able to communicate with your chosen penfriend online. Ask your parents first! It is always exciting to receive mail so it might be more fun to stick to letters.

Photograph frames

Soccer frame

What you will need
★ corrugated cardboard
★ ruler and pencil
★ newspaper
★ glue
★ ping pong ball
★ craft knife
★ paints and brush
★ black felt-tip pen

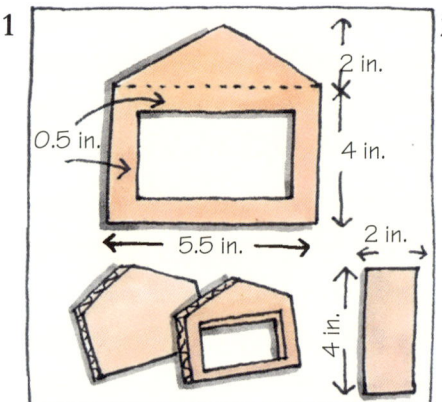

1 Cut the card into two frame shapes. Cut a rectangular hole in the top piece. Also cut out a back flap.

2 Glue small torn pieces of newspaper around all the cut edges. Leave to dry.

3 Glue around the top, bottom, and one side of the top piece. Press down on to back piece.

4 Use craft knife for cutting. Cut the ball in two. Hold in position on the frame and draw around it. Cut lightly inside the line.

5 Paint the frame in your team colors. Paint the back and the flap. Leave it to dry.

6 Draw football markings with felt-tip. Glue around the edge of the ball. Push firmly into place. Score the top of the flap, fold it, and glue it on to the back.

30

Folded frames

Here is a simple way to display your favorite TV characters, sports, or pop stars. You can update the pictures by sticking new ones over the top of the old. Cut some card stock or paper according to the size of your pictures. Make small ones to put in your pocket or bag.

Fold the card stock in two and stick cut-out pictures on both sides.

Stick a piece of tape inside to keep it standing up. Stick pictures on the front and back.

Zig zag

What you will need
- ★ stiff colored paper
- ★ ruler and pencil
- ★ scissors
- ★ pictures
- ★ two 6-in. lengths of ribbon
- ★ sticky tape and glue

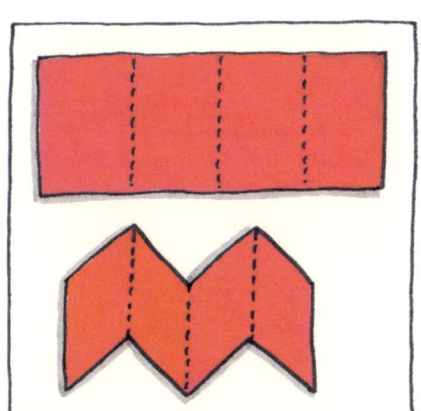

Measure and cut out the paper according to the size of your pictures. Divide into four and fold as shown.

Cut out and glue pictures on to each of the four surfaces.

Tape a length of ribbon to each end, on the back. Tie them up to carry with you.

Friendship diary

Make a diary with your best friend. Fill it with pockets, and fold-out pages. Decorate it with stickers. You can collect all sorts of bits and pieces to add to your diary.

What you will need
★ thin card stock
★ sticky tape
★ paper
★ scissors
★ felt-tip pens
★ elastic bands
★ ruler
★ pencil
★ stickers
★ envelope

photos   maps   old tickets

Card cover

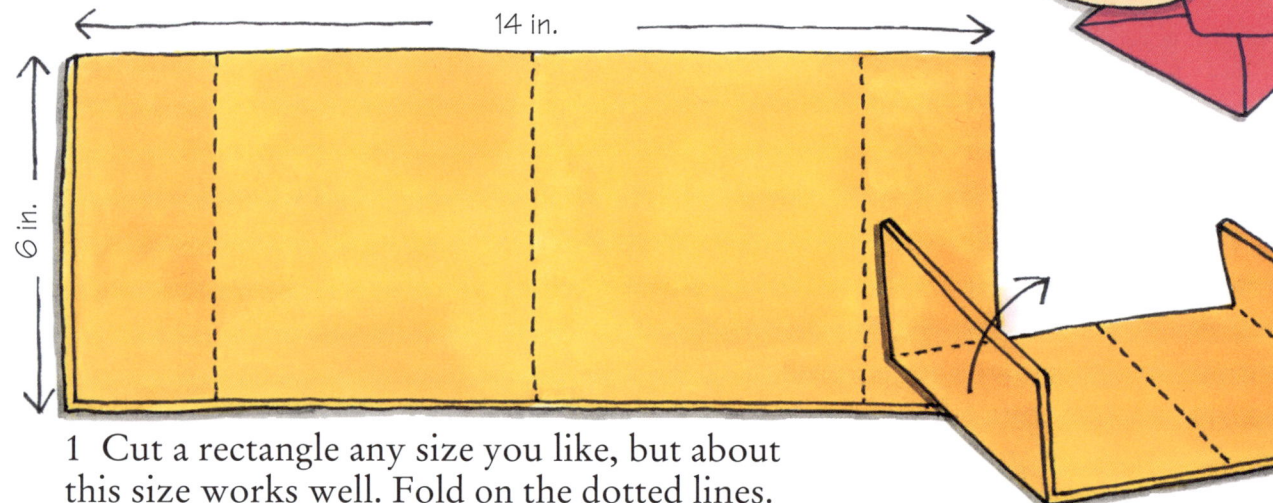

1 Cut a rectangle any size you like, but about this size works well. Fold on the dotted lines.

2 Fold the flaps over.

Pages

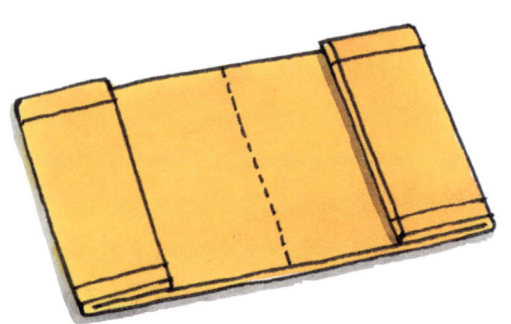

3 Tape the flaps at top and bottom.

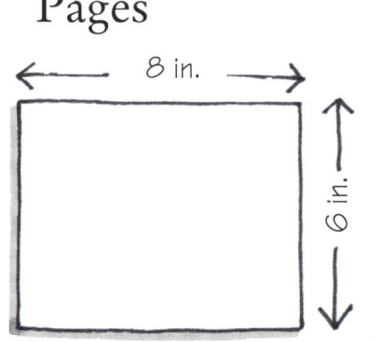

Cut paper pages to fit inside.

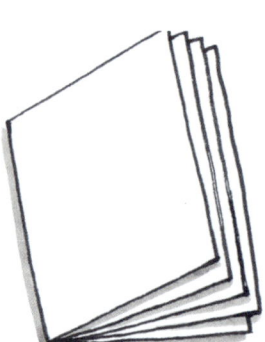

Fold the pages.

32

Put the pages inside the cover. Open the pages and slip a thick rubber band around the center of them and the cover.

Add a paper pocket.

Close and keep closed with another rubber band. Slip a pen or pencil in the band.

Decorate the cover with stickers and messages—PRIVATE, KEEP OUT, TOM'S DIARY. Tape an envelope on the back to keep things in.

Make and decorate page markers.

Important information

Here is a list of some things you might like to put in your diary:
- ★ name and age
- ★ address
- ★ telephone number
- ★ school
- ★ names of friends with addresses and phone numbers
- ★ favorite things—food, sports team, bands, books, and so on
- ★ map of where you live
- ★ zodiac sign (see page 42)
- ★ you could write in code

Pages with tabs

Fold two pieces of paper to form four pages. Leave the bottom one. Cut a strip 0.5 in. wide, one quarter of the way up from the bottom on the next page. Do the same on the next but cut it to half way up the page. Finally cut a strip three-quarters of the way up the top page.

Color the strips all the way along the page edges.

Friendship

Little Clotilda
Well and hearty
Thought she'd like
To give a party
But as her friends
Were shy and wary
Nobody came
But her own canary

"Dogs are a man's best friend."

A friend in need is a friend indeed!

Tongue twister
Freddie's friend Eddie phoned
For Freddie to fetch fruit from the farm
Of the famous French farmer.

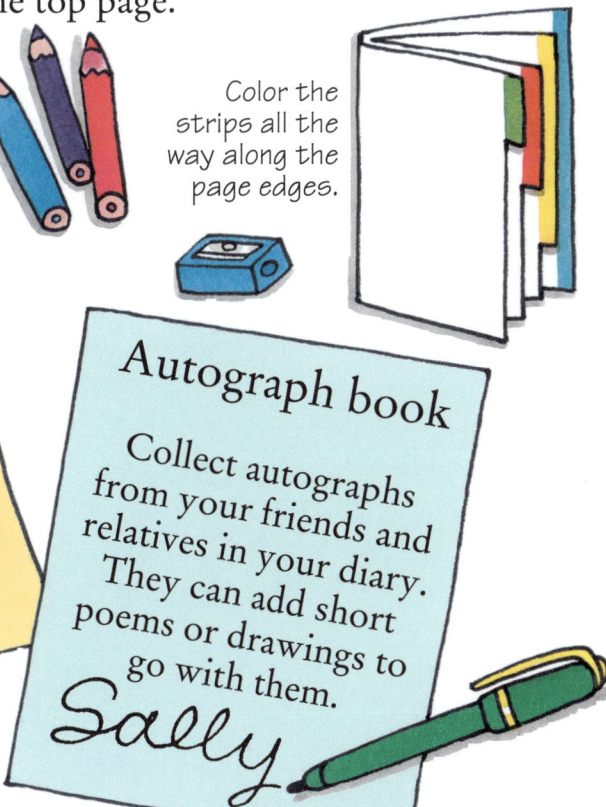

Autograph book

Collect autographs from your friends and relatives in your diary. They can add short poems or drawings to go with them.

Sally

Friendship cards

Making a personal card for a friend is very worthwhile. It's great fun to make something that you know they will find funny or lovely and especially for them!

As well as cards for birthdays, there are lots of other times you could give a friend a card: Valentine's cards, Missing You cards, Welcome Home cards, and Good Luck or Well Done cards. Here are some ideas you might like to try.

Keep a small collection of old, unwanted photos, magazines, colored and patterned papers.

Window card

What you will need
★ 9.5 in. x 6 in. piece of paper
★ pencil and ruler
★ craft knife
★ colored pens or pencils
★ photograph

1 Fold paper in two, then open again.

Draw a rectangle as shown. Cut along the top, bottom, and central lines only.

2 Open the window "flaps."

Draw around inside the rectangle with a pencil on to the bottom sheet.

3 Decorate the front of the card.

Draw or stick a photo of yourself or yourself and your friend inside the pencil rectangle.

Fancy cards

Shaped messages

Draw bold outline shapes on to stiff colored paper. Cut out. Write a message on the back.

Sweetie cards

Cut a square card from stiff, brightly colored paper. Draw the initial of your friend, or a heart, in pencil on the front. Carefully cover the shape in glue and stick on small candies.

Warning! Do not eat the sweets if they have glue on them!

My hero

Stick a picture of your friend's head on to a favorite sports person.

Collage cards

Make a collage of drawings or favorite pictures torn or cut out of magazines. Stick them on to colored paper.

Spot the difference

Can you spot 11 differences between these two pictures?

36

Flapjacks

What you will need to make 10 bars
★ 1/2 cp + 2 tsp. soft light brown sugar
★ 3/4 cup butter or margarine
★ 2 tsp corn syrup
★ 2 cups porridge oats
★ small teaspoon ground ginger
★ wooden spoon
★ heavy-based saucepan
★ 8 in. square shallow baking tin

1

Stir occasionally.

Warning! Ask a grown-up to help with the heating.

Put the sugar, butter or margarine, and syrup into the saucepan and heat gently until dissolved.

2

Remove from the heat. Add the porridge oats and ginger. Stir them together.

3

Pre-heat the oven to 300°F. Butter the baking tin. Press the mixture evenly into the tin.

4

After cutting leave in tin until cold.

Bake in the center of the oven for 45 minutes. Cool for 10 minutes before cutting into bars.

Clubs

Forming a club with a group of friends is really fun. But be careful not to exclude others or make them feel left out and unwanted.

Club name

The first thing to do when you start a club is to think of a name. Something simple is best which can be made into a symbol (an easily recognized picture or sign). If your club has a particular interest, such as football or animals, then that can help you decide.

Silver Star

Black Cat

Football Five

Green Leaf

Symbol

A symbol can be used on badges, membership cards, writing paper and made into a stamp using potato prints.

Tape a safety-pin on the back.

Cut badges from card—one for each member. They can be circles, squares, or triangles.

To make a membership card, cut a piece of thin card stock into a credit card size. Draw the symbol and club name on one side. Write the member's name on the back. Include a thumbprint.

If the club is a secret one, wear your badge inside your jacket or pin it inside your bag.

You could even have a potato print tattoo!

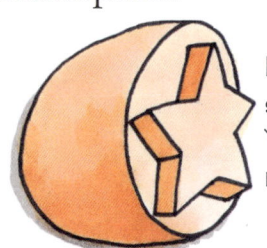

Make a potato cut of your symbol to use as a stamp. You can print it on paper for messages or a newsletter.

Clothes

Members of a club could decide to wear certain clothes or colors, like a team. You could decide to wear something special—a cap, scarf, or bracelet made of a strand of yarn, or a friendship bracelet in special colors (see page 44). You must wear these at meetings.

Wear a certain color yarn bracelet or your badge to give a message to another member, like

★ See you at the meeting today!
★ I need to give you club news!

You could have secret signs to say "hello" to another member, like scratching your nose, or rubbing your ear, or a cough. You could write messages too in code.

Rules

Make a small book or card with the club rules and ideals or aims written in it. Find out about issues you are interested in.

Meetings

Think of a PASSWORD and remember to say it when you meet. Hold meetings regularly to discuss what you want to do as a group, like play a game of football, visit a museum, write to a fan club, or just have a good time. You could swap pictures, magazines and news about your special interest.

CLUB INTERESTS
Environment and conservation
Less pollution and cars, anti-smoking, save the forest, save trees
Football
Favorite clubs, rules, dates of matches, match scores
Bands
Best bands, collect photos and facts. Plan to go to a concert.
OR Collections, Cars, Dance, Drawing, Tennis.

Nail painting

You only have to look at all the wonderful colors and finishes of nail polish to make you want to start painting your nails. So stop biting them and get started!

Manicure

Before you polish your nails give them a quick manicure. File your nails with an emery board. It is best to file from the edges to the center of your nails.

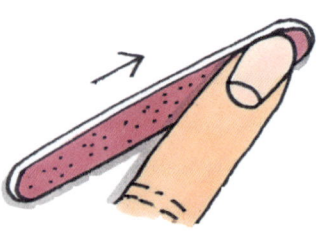
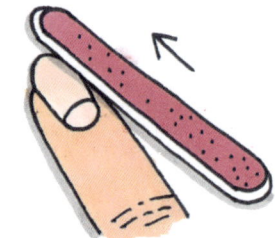

Next rub some cuticle cream (or hand cream) into the cuticles, this is the hard skin at the base of the nails, to soften them. Gently push back the cuticle with a Q-tip.

For a special occasion try different colors and patterns. Here are some ideas.

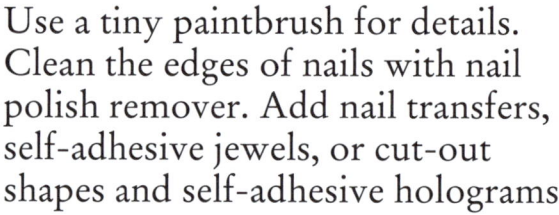

Use a tiny paintbrush for details. Clean the edges of nails with nail polish remover. Add nail transfers, self-adhesive jewels, or cut-out shapes and self-adhesive holograms.

Polishing

Carefully paint a thin layer of nail polish on to your nails starting with a stroke in the center. Leave to dry before applying a second coat.

 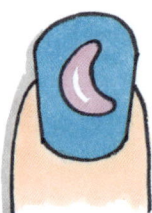 

Card games

Card games are great fun. Take a pack of cards anywhere and you can play loads of games on your own or with friends. These ones are for two players although Slapjack can also be played with more than two.

Slapjack

Deal out all the cards between the players. Each player puts his/her cards in a neat pile face down in front of him/her. Do not look at them!

Take it in turns to place the top card of your pile face up in the middle of the table, making one new pile. Continue until one player turns up a Jack.

Each player tries to be the first to slap a hand on the Jack and shout "Slapjack!" The winner gets the whole pile. Then carry on until one person has won the whole pack.

Three and four

Using one pack of cards (no jokers) deal seven cards each. Put the rest in a pile face down with the top card face up next to it. This is a throwaway pile. The aim is to collect either:

1 Three or four cards of the same number—four 8s or three 10s and/or

2 A run of three or four cards of the same suit—e.g. 2, 3, 4 of diamonds

Take turns to pick up the top card from either the face-down pile or the throwaway pile. You can keep it or throw it away. If you keep it you have to throw away another card from your hand (so you always have seven cards). If the center pile finishes turn it over and use it again. The winner is the first to put down a completed collection.

Signs of the zodiac

The ancient Greeks studied the stars and their position in the heavens and their influence on people's lives. They named the twelve signs of the zodiac after important Greek mythological characters. Some people still believe that we are influenced by a particular sign. Your birthday tells you which sign you are.

ARIES
21 MARCH
– 20 APRIL

TAURUS
21 APRIL
– 21 MAY

GEMINI
22 MAY
– 21 JUNE

CANCER
22 JUNE
– 23 JULY

LEO
24 JULY–
23 AUGUST

VIRGO
24 AUGUST
– 23 SEPT

LIBRA
24 SEPT
– 23 OCT

SCORPIO
24 OCT
– 22 NOV

SAGITTARIUS
23 NOV
– 21 DEC

CAPRICORN
22 DEC
– 20 JAN

AQUARIUS
21 JAN
– 19 FEB

PISCES
20 FEB
– 20 MARCH

Jewels of the month

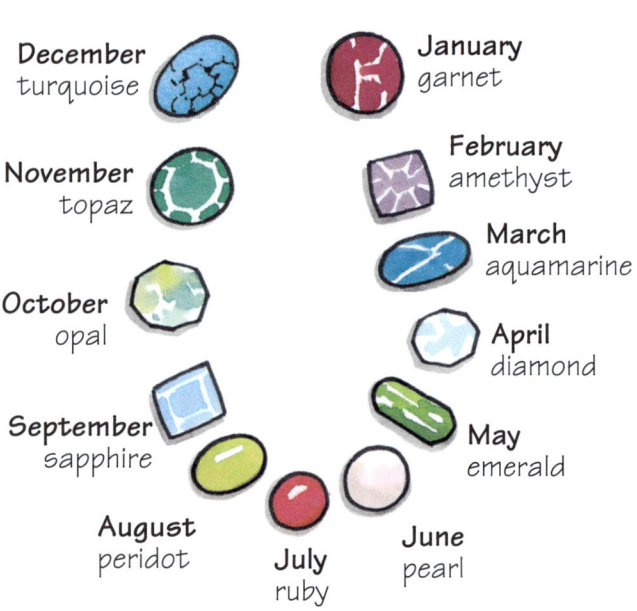

December turquoise
November topaz
October opal
September sapphire
August peridot
July ruby
June pearl
May emerald
April diamond
March aquamarine
February amethyst
January garnet

Flowers of the month

December narcissus
November chrysanthemum
October marigold
September aster
August gladioli
July larkspur
June rose
May lily of the valley
April sweetpea
March daffodil
February violet
January carnation

Chinese new year

For the Chinese, each year is named after one of twelve creatures. Each creature is supposed to have different characteristics which pass on to those born in that year. Which year were you born in? Are you like other people born in the same animal year?

Years of the Rat
1924   1960   1996
1936   1972   2008
1948   1984

Years of the Horse
1930   1966   2002
1942   1978   2014
1954   1990

Years of the Ox
1925   1961   1997
1937   1973   2009
1949   1985

Years of the Goat
1931   1967   2003
1943   1979   2015
1955   1991

Years of the Tiger
1926   1962   1998
1938   1974   2010
1950   1986

Years of the Monkey
1932   1968   2004
1944   1980   2016
1956   1992

Years of the Rabbit
1927   1963   1999
1939   1975   2011
1951   1987

Years of the Rooster
1933   1969   2005
1945   1981   2017
1957   1993

Years of the Dragon
1928   1964   2000
1940   1976   2012
1952   1988

Years of the Dog
1934   1970   2006
1946   1982   2018
1958   1994

Years of the Snake
1929   1965   2001
1941   1977   2013
1953   1989

Years of the Pig
1935   1971   2007
1947   1983   2019
1959   1995

Friendship bracelets

These bracelets are made by knotting strands of colored embroidery thread together. The more threads you use the wider the bracelet will be. You can use two of each color as if it were one thread.

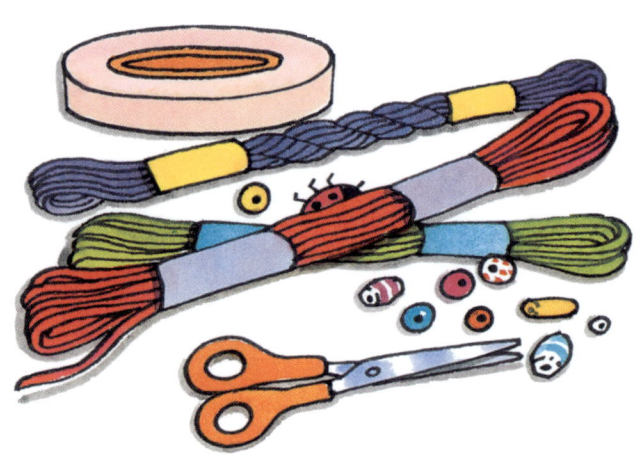

What you will need
- ★ 27.5 in. lengths of three different-colored threads
- ★ sticky tape
- ★ scissors

1
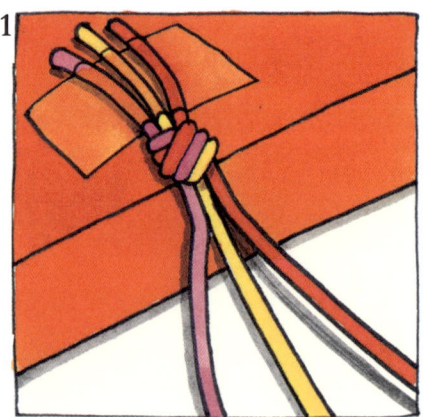
Knot the ends of the threads together 2 in. from the ends. Tape them firmly to a table edge.

2
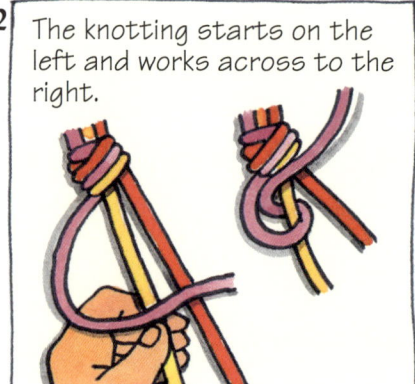
The knotting starts on the left and works across to the right.

Now make a row of four knots all with the left thread. First knot around the middle thread, twice.

3
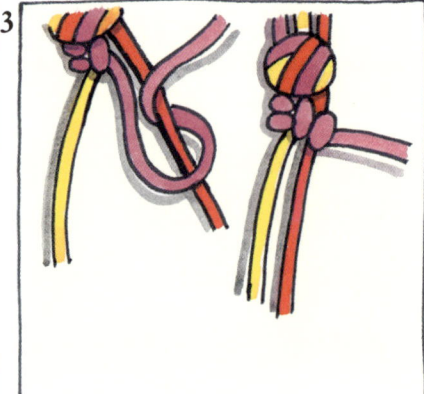
Next make two knots around the right thread. Push the knots up to the top but not too tight.

4
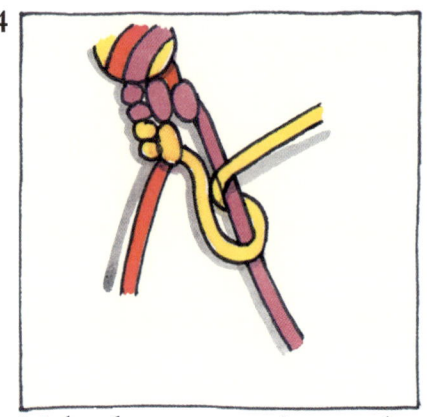
Make the next row in exactly the same way. Use the next color which is now on the left.

5
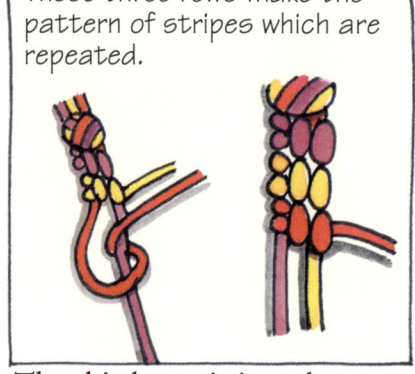
These three rows make the pattern of stripes which are repeated.

The third row is just the same. Knot with the third color (now on the left).

6

Carry on until the bracelet is long enough.

Tie the loose ends in a knot. Remove from tape and tie around your friend's wrist. Trim the ends.

Fancy bracelets

Once you've got the hang of making the simplest kind of bracelet (on page 44), you can start to make fancier, wider ones.

The method is always the same—two knots with each thread from left to right. But now use four, five, or six threads. Create different patterns by using several threads of the same color and one or more of another color.

Wear a bracelet on your ankle too!

You can braid the ends if you like.

Make a braid for your friend's glasses.

Beaded bracelets

Thread a bead on to the thread that you are about to knot. Carry on as usual. Space the beads evenly—perhaps just on one color as it comes up for knotting.

There are many variations. Try different color combinations and endings to your braid. Finish off with a bead or a feather.

Hairbraiding

What you will need
★ small piece of paper
★ three colors of embroidery thread three times as long as the strand of hair

1. Make a small hole in the paper. Pull a strand of hair through and dampen it.

2. Tie three threads to the top of the hair. Wind around the hair, (covering ends of thread).

3. Tear the paper off when finished.

Just before the end of the strand of hair, tie the hair and threads in a knot.

45

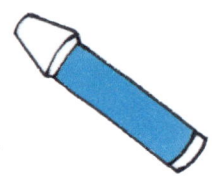

Yummy dips

Serve these delicious dips when your friends come over. They can be eaten with pieces of carrot, sticks of celery, bread sticks (grissini), and tortilla chips.

Curried dip

What you will need
- ★ small carton of crème fraîche, sour cream, or plain yogurt
- ★ 1 teaspoon curry powder

Spoon the sour cream or yogurt into a bowl and stir in the curry powder.

Avocado dip

What you will need
- ★ 1 ripe avocado
- ★ 1 cup cream cheese
- ★ 1/2 cup + 2 tsp double cream
- ★ 1 teaspoon lemon juice
- ★ pepper and salt

Warning! Ask a grown-up to help with the cutting.

1. Cut the avocado in half and remove the stone. Scoop the flesh out and put in a bowl.

2. Add the cream cheese, cream, and lemon juice. Mash together with a fork.

3. Season with a little pepper and salt. Spoon the dip into a serving bowl.

Best friends heart pendant

What you will need
- ★ corrugated cardboard
- ★ tracing paper and pencil
- ★ craft knife
- ★ red and blue paper
- ★ glue
- ★ scissors
- ★ sequins
- ★ compass
- ★ two 35.5 in. lengths of yarn

template

1

Trace the outline of the heart template on to the cardboard (see instructions on page 4). Cut out two halves.

2
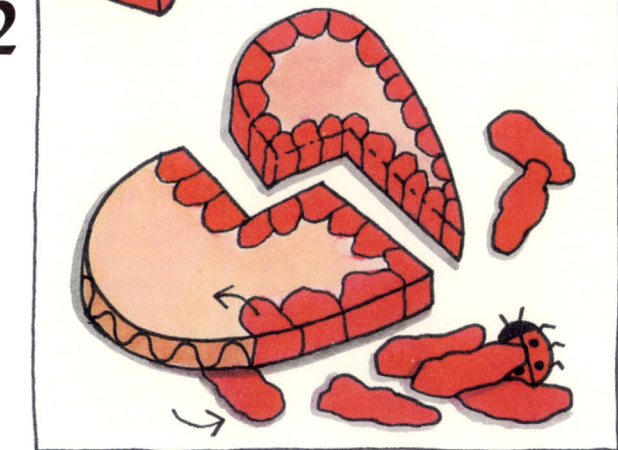

Tear red paper into small pieces and glue around the edges. Leave to dry.

3

Glue on to both sides of cardboard halves.

Using the template again, cut out two smaller heart shapes in blue paper. Cut into halves.

4
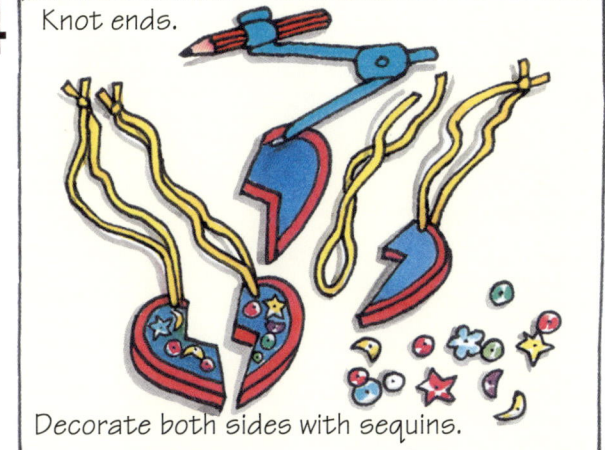

Knot ends.

Decorate both sides with sequins.

Push the pointed end of the compass through tops of halves and thread yarn through the holes.

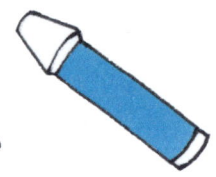

Fundraising

On these pages, you will find lots of ideas on ways to help raise money for your school at a Summer Fair or Christmas Bazaar. You could also ask if you can set up a special stall to collect money for a charity you feel strongly about.

What you will need
- small table
- two chairs
- notice and means of hanging it up
- box for money
- bags
- labels and pens

What to sell

If you have some toys, stationery (small notebooks, pens, erasers), or jewelery, group them together. Large baskets look good. Remember to decide on prices before you set up your stall and mark the prices clearly on the goods or make notices. You can always drop your prices towards the end of the fair.

Small bags of popcorn are always popular. Make as much as you possibly can! Single flapjacks (see page 37), cookies, and chocolate crispies also sell well.

Fruit stall

If the weather is hot and sunny, people will gladly buy cool slices of watermelon or pineapple. You will need a cutting board, a sharp knife (take care!), a tray to put the slices on, cocktail sticks to serve with, and lots of paper towels. Slice as you sell (to keep fresh) and, if you have any melons or pineapples left over, sell them whole or halved to take home.

Three guessing games

You can have one of these on your stall, or you can walk around asking people their guesses. Prepare a sheet beforehand with two columns: one for the name and email address (or phone number) and one for the guess. The winner wins the item.

Lucky dip

This is very popular with small children—you'll have a line all day! Collect small inexpensive toys from friends, or spend a little money on small party gifts. Wrap them in paper. Fill a laundry basket or (clean) plastic garbage can with shredded newspaper. Mix in the surprises.

Other ideas

Instead of selling things, you could offer a service, like nail painting (see page 40), hairbraiding (see page 45), and face painting. These are all good fun and money spinners!

Plan ahead! Get together your equipment and choose three or four simple designs the customers can choose. Have lots of volunteers to help. Don't spend too long on each customer or you'll end up with unhappy customers and very little money. Keep it as simple as possible.

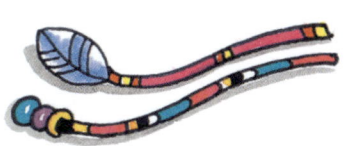

Pasta jewelery

Children love making their own necklaces from different-shaped pasta (with holes). Paint some first and organize into different boxes. All they need then is some string.

Fortune teller

Once you've made one of these, you can make others with different patterns on the outside, letters or pictures instead of colors inside, and lots of different messages. Messages can be silly, rude, a joke, or something nice. They could even be a dare (something your friend must do).

Some ideas for decorating your fortune teller.

What you will need
★ 8 in. square white paper
★ felt-tip pens

1 Fold the paper into four. Open and fold each corner into the center.

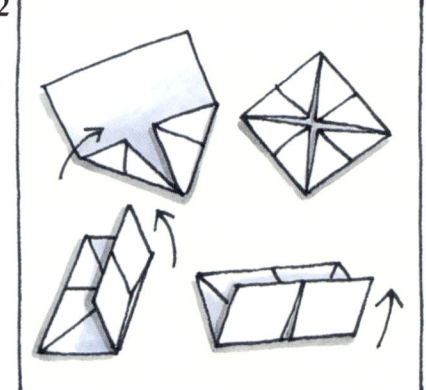

2 Turn over and fold each corner into the center. Fold the square into a rectangle.

3 Open the square and lift up each flap. Write two messages under each flap (eight in all).

4 Turn over and decorate. Close the flaps and color the eight triangles in different colors.

5 Put a forefinger and thumb of each hand into the four pockets and close the teller.

Now you're ready to play! Ask a friend to say a number. Open and close the teller, counting. Then ask for a color. Open and read out the message.

 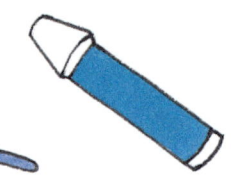

Before you begin

It's great to be outdoors on a sunny day but you can even find things to do and discover in cold or rainy weather. And at night you can stargaze. When you are out in a park or garden, in the countryside or on the beach, see if you can spot insects, animals, and birds, or any signs of them. Some of the ideas on the following pages use things you can collect outdoors, like shells, pine cones, and daisies. Be careful what you collect and don't take too much.

Some basic tools and materials:
paint and brushes
varnish and glue
scissors and craft knife
paper and card
colored pencils and felt-tip pens

- Always take great care with sharp tools such as scissors, needles and knives.
- Always cover work surfaces with newspaper before you start to paint or varnish your work.
- When using a craft knife always cut away from hands. Use thick card stock or something similar under whatever you are cutting. Cut slowly and lightly several times.
- Wash your hands and wear an apron before preparing food.
- You can find most of the materials used in this book, like cardboard boxes, for free, or you will already have them at home. Recycle wire coat-hangers, old buttons, newspapers, and foil food containers.

 **This symbol is to remind you to take care when you use a craft knife.**

 This daisy will be hidden on pages 53 to 74. See if you can spot it.

Weather forecasts

Studying the weather has always been important for farmers, sailors and pilots. Today, scientists called "meteorologists" give us weather forecasts. They study clouds, the direction of the wind, the temperature, and the pressure of the Earth's atmosphere. They use satellites, computers, and other up-to-the-minute technology.

You can study the weather too. Try keeping a simple weather diary. Note sunny days, rain, the shape of the clouds, the strength of the wind, and the temperature (if you have a thermometer).

Here are some traditional ways you can foretell the weather.

Seaweed
Hang some up and if it is soft and limp, it means rain is coming. If it goes dry and crisp, it will be fine. This is because the salt in the seaweed absorbs moisture from the air.

Pine cones
Pine cones can also tell you if it will be fine or wet. If the pine cone is open, it will be fine. If it is closed, it will be wet.

Weather vanes
You often see weather vanes on house roofs in the country or on the top of church spires. The vane moves in the wind and points to the direction from which it is coming.

Cloud shapes
The three main types of cloud are called by their Latin names: Cumulus (heap), Stratus (flat), and Cirrus (curl of hair).

Cumulus—white fluffy clouds. Means fair weather, but larger dark ones usually bring bad weather.

Stratus—layer of thin, pale, grey clouds covering the whole sky. Usually means drizzle.

Cirrus—streaky, wispy clouds. Means windy weather and possibly storms to come.

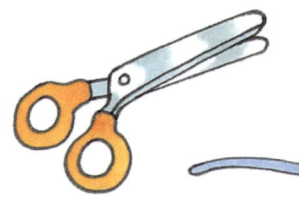
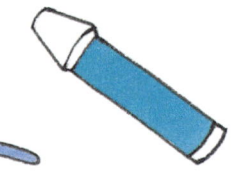

Hats

You will need a hat when you are outdoors, especially in the sun or rain. You can make these hats yourself. Once you have made the basic shape, you can decorate them however you like.

What you will need
★ scissors
★ newspaper
★ sticky tape and glue
★ thin card stock
★ pencil and ruler
★ compass
★ plastic bags (cut open)
★ ribbon
★ hole punch

Warning! Never put a plastic bag over your head. Cut along the sides and open before using.

Newspaper sun hat

Cut a 15 x 15 in. square of newspaper. Fold it in half. Fold the edges up 1 in.

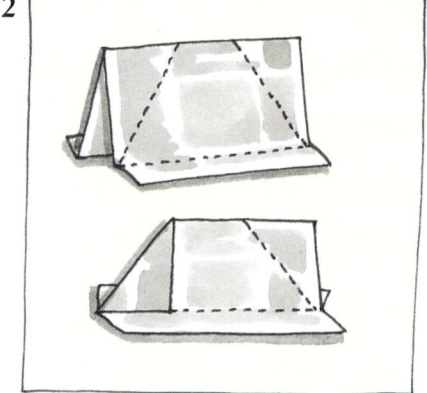

Flatten out the edges again. Then fold down the corners to the fold line.

Tape down the folded corners. Fold up the brim and open out the hat.

Conical rain hat

1 Mark center point.

2

3 Tape two lengths of ribbon inside.

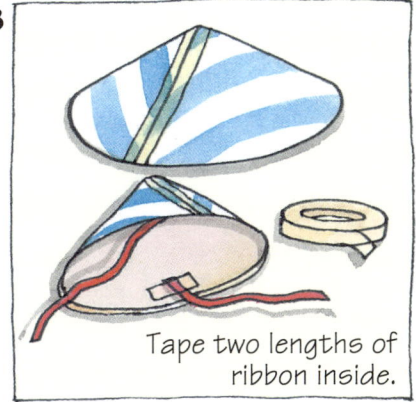

Draw and cut out a large circle from thin card stock. Glue over an open plastic bag.

Trim the plastic along the edge of the card stock. Cut a slit from the edge to the center point.

Pull to form a shallow cone. Tape together inside and out.

Shady brim

1

2

3

Draw and cut out a large circle from thin card stock. Draw a smaller circle inside to fit on head.

Cut out the center circle. Cut different colored plastic bags into strips.

Make small holes around the brim with a hole punch or scissors. Push the strips through and knot.

Outdoor games

These games can be played by any child no matter their gender.

Leap frog

For any number of players. This is best played on grass for a soft landing.
The first player bends over, steadying their legs with their hands, their head tucked in.

The next player takes a short run, places their hands on the first player's back, and leaps over them with their legs wide apart, like a frog.

This player now runs a little way and bends down to be jumped over. Any number of players can play, each bending over after leaping.

French skipping

You will need a long loop of elastic and three or more players.
Two players stand about one yard apart, facing each other with the elastic loop round their ankles.

The third player stands inside the loop and they all recite a rhyme (see below) while the player jumps in and out of the loop.

At the end of the rhyme, the player jumps on top of the loop.

They all then repeat the rhyme, moving the elastic loop higher up their legs each time.

If the jumping player makes a mistake, they are out.

Diagram of rhyme
X is a foot.

 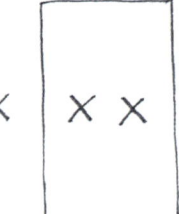 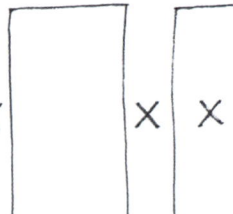 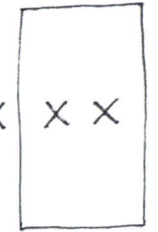 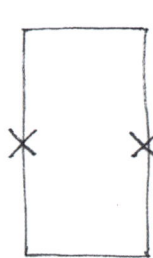

England　　Ireland　　Scotland　　Wales　　inside　　outside　　inside　　on

Sevens

For this game you need a rubber ball or tennis ball, a wall, and flat ground where the ball will bounce evenly.

The idea is to bounce the ball seven different ways, seven times each, and to catch it each time.

Here are some ways, but you can make up some more yourself. If you drop the ball, you must begin that set of seven again. Remember, do these each *seven* times!

1 Throw it straight against the wall and catch it, no bounce.

2 Throw it against the wall, let it bounce once before you catch it.

3 Bounce it on the ground first and catch it when it bounces off the wall.

4 Throw it straight against the wall and catch it in your left hand.

5 Throw it straight against the wall and catch it in your right hand.

6 Throw it with your left hand under your raised left leg and catch it again with your left hand.

7 Throw it with your right hand under your raised right leg and catch it again with your right hand.

Piggy in the middle

You need three players and a ball.
The players stand in a row, one at each end and one in the middle, as far apart as they want.

The outside players throw the ball to each other whilst the "Piggy" or middle player tries to catch it.

If the "Piggy" catches the ball, they change places with the player who threw it.

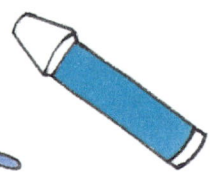

Picnic food

Everything seems to taste nicer outdoors. Perhaps it's just because fresh air makes us hungrier? You can make these recipes in advance and freeze them if necessary. Remember to thaw them out a few hours before you need them.

Sandwich loaf

This is delicious and looks wonderful with all the different layers.

What you will need
★ one large unsliced loaf
★ fillings such as cream cheese, peanut butter, ham, egg salad
★ bread knife and board
★ tin foil

1. Cut the loaf into six slices, lengthways! Spread with the five different fillings.

2. Put together and wrap in tin foil. Put something heavy on top. Put it in the fridge.

3. When cold, and the slices are stuck together, unwrap. Slice the normal way and eat!

Chocolate bars

What you will need
- ★ 1 3/4 cups + 2 tbsp graham crackers
- ★ 1/4 cup mixed chopped nuts
- ★ 1/2 cup raisins
- ★ 2 tablespoons corn syrup
- ★ 1/4 cup + 1 tbsp butter or margarine
- ★ 1/2 cup plain chocolate
- ★ paper or plastic bag
- ★ rolling-pin
- ★ mixing bowl
- ★ small saucepan
- ★ wooden or metal spoon
- ★ greased 7 in. square tin

Warning! Ask an adult to help you with the heating.

1

Crush the biscuits in a bag with a rolling pin. Put the crackers, nuts, and raisins in the bowl.

2

Melt the syrup, butter or margarine, and chocolate gently in a pan over a low heat.

3

Place in fridge for two hours. Cut into bars.
Pour into the bowl and mix together. Put in a tin and press down with a spoon.

Elderflower cordial

What you will need
- ★ 2 1/4 cups of sugar
- ★ 2 1/2 cups of water
- ★ juice of 1 lemon
- ★ 8-10 elderflower heads
- ★ saucepan and wooden spoon
- ★ colander and clean plastic bottles

Warning! Ask an adult to help you with the heating.

1

Dissolve the sugar in the water over a low heat. Add the lemon juice and boil for 30 seconds.

2

Take off the heat. Wash and drain the flower heads and add them. Leave overnight.

3

Don't fill the bottles you want to freeze to the top.
Strain through a colander. Pour into bottles and keep in the fridge. To drink, dilute with water to taste.

Spotting creepy crawlies

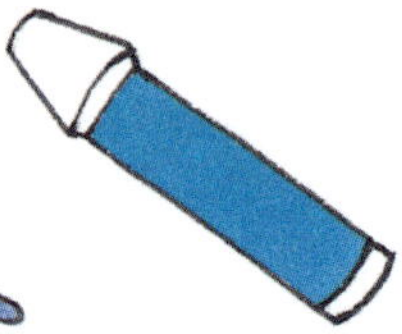

Look for these in the garden or park. Make your own chart and tick the box where you found them. Try this at different times of the year and see if there are any changes.

creepy crawlies	under a stone	in the grass	on a bush or tree	on a path
ladybird			✓ 3	
snail	✓			
ant		✓ 5		✓ 8
woodlouse	✓ 7			
caterpillar				
butterfly				
worm	✓ 3			
spider			✓ 2	
earwig				
beetle		✓ 1	✓ 2	

Add more creepy crawlies and places on your chart. Have a competition with a friend and see how many you can find.

two inside a sandwich

on my T-shirt

in my shoe!

under my bed!

Don't capture or touch the creatures you find. Sometimes they have very delicate legs! Just leave them where they are.

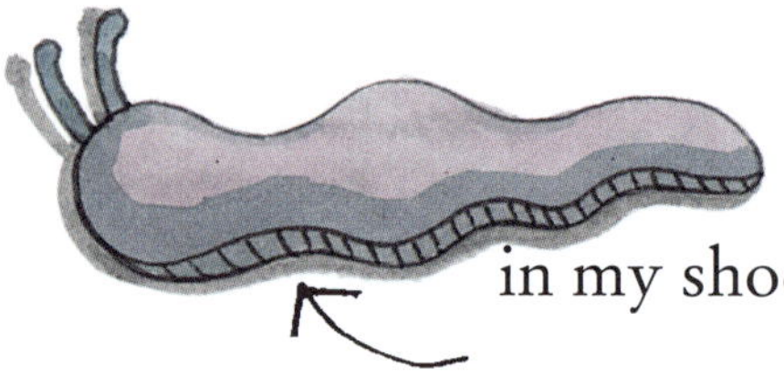

Wind chime

These are also called "wind bells." They are clusters of small pieces of metal, glass, pottery, bamboo, or seashells that tinkle when the wind blows through them.

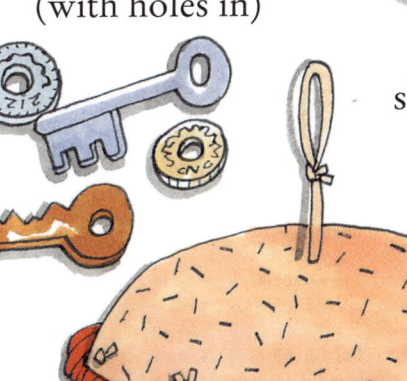

metal bottle tops (and foil milk tops)

Bamboo chime

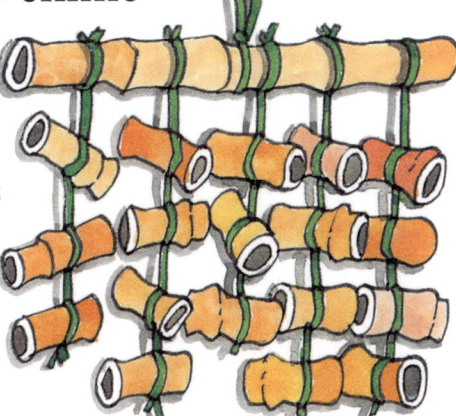

Make chimes out of small pieces of bamboo.

old keys and coins (with holes in)

shells

Basket and bottle tops

What you will need
★ small straw basket
★ thin string
★ darning needle
★ small light objects which sound nice when jangled

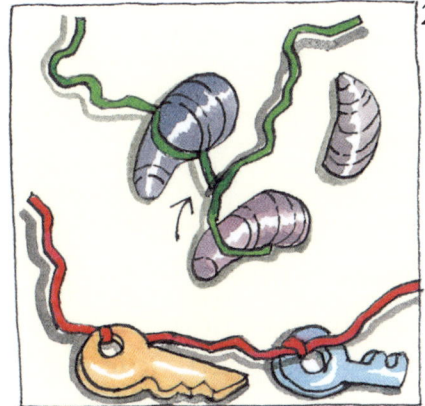

1 Tie your collected bits on lengths of string. Tie round them or through their holes.

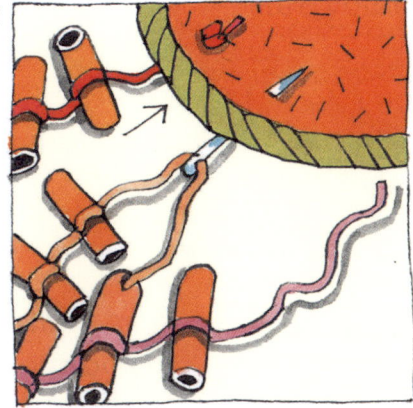

2 Thread the strings through the basket with a darning needle. Knot the ends.

3 Hang your wind chime where it will catch the breeze. Then you'll hear it!

Plaster plaque

This is an attractive and unusual way to keep and display all the bits and pieces you collect outdoors. Make one as a memento of a day out or a vacation. Take care as plaster will break if you drop it.

What you will need
★ water
★ cup
★ large bowl
★ plaster of Paris
★ plastic bowl or box
★ two pencils or sticks
★ nature collection
★ cord or string
★ pencil to write with

Note that plaster is cheapest bought in bulk from a building supply store.

1 Have your collection ready before you start.

Pour one cup of cold water into the bowl. Sprinkle two cups of plaster into the water. Leave for two minutes.

2 Carefully stir it with your hand to mix well and remove lumps. Leave for four minutes.

3 Press pencils into the top of the mixture to make holes. Turn them regularly.

Pour into the box. Tap the sides gently to release any air bubbles. Get ready to put your collection in as the plaster starts to set in just a few minutes.

4 Remove pencils.

Quickly arrange the collection, pressing down gently. Fill any gaps with the smallest items.

5

Leave to set hard for thirty minutes. Carefully remove the plaster from the box.

6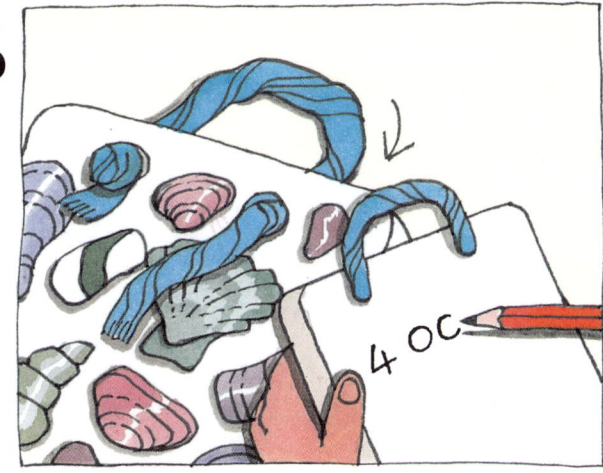

Thread cord through the holes and knot the ends. Holding carefully, write the date and any other details on the back. Hang up.

If you like, you can dye the plaster with a few drops of ink or food coloring at step 2.

You might even find the cord on the beach as well!

List of things you could collect

stones and pebbles   feathers
pine cones   dried leaves
seeds   nuts
shells   fossils
twigs

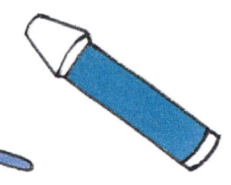

Falling leaves

Each of these leaves has a pair except one.
Can you spot the odd one out?

Tracks

When you are out, especially after rain or snow, look out for animal and bird tracks. If you find a good clear one in mud, you can make a plaster cast of it. Use the instructions on page 62 for mixing the plaster.

What you will need
★ cardboard
★ water
★ plaster of Paris
★ pencil

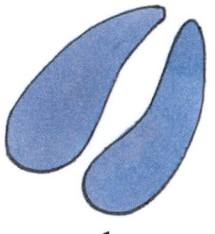

Roe deer

Rabbit
Tracks show little details as the soles are hairy. Look for short front feet and long back feet.

Fox
Four toes and prominent claws.

Squirrel
Most rodents, including mice, voles, and rats have four toes on the front feet and five on the longer back feet.

Cat
Four toes but no claws as these are pulled in when the cat is walking.

Dog
Similar to foxes. Vary in size but are wider than foxes.

Track cast

Wild duck

1 No gaps

Make a "box" around the track with cardboard strips pushed into the ground.

2

Clear away any twigs or leaves. Mix the plaster (see page 62) and pour in slowly.

3

When set, remove the card "box" and lift up plaster cast. Write on the name and date.

 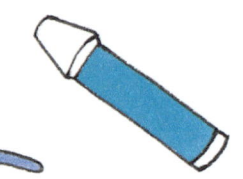

Growing things

Sunflowers

Plant a sunflower seed in a sunny spot in the garden or in a pot in a sunny place.

Water it regularly. You may need to tie it to a stake, especially on a high, windy balcony. Sunflowers can grow over 10 feet tall!

You could have a race with a friend and see whose grows the tallest.

Lettuces and radishes

Nothing tastes better than vegetables you have grown yourself!

Radishes grow very quickly. You should be able to eat some types three weeks after sowing the seeds.

Herbs grow quickly too and you can eat nasturtium and pansy flowers!

Sow the seeds in a window-box, pot or garden.

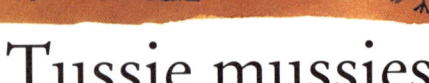

Tussie mussies

What you will need

★ flowers and herbs
★ yarn
★ paper doily
★ silver foil

If you grow some small flowers and herbs, here is a pretty way of making posies to give to a friend or your teacher.

Start with one flower and arrange the other flowers and herbs around it.

Tie each circle of flowers and leaves with yarn.

Push the stems through the doily. Twist foil around the stems.

The night sky

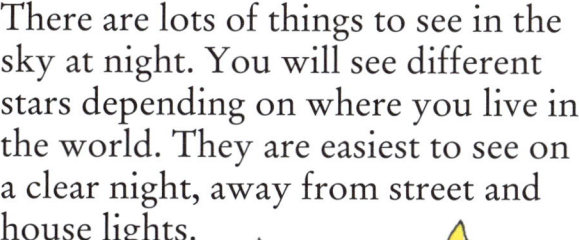

There are lots of things to see in the sky at night. You will see different stars depending on where you live in the world. They are easiest to see on a clear night, away from street and house lights.

Our sun and solar system belong to a family of stars called the Milky Way galaxy. It has one hundred, thousand, million stars!

Stars form from the collapse of clouds of gas and dust in space. They appear to twinkle because their light wobbles as it shines through the earth's atmosphere.

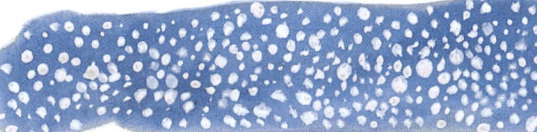

Shooting stars are meteors or rocks burning as they enter the earth's atmosphere.

Patterns of stars are given special names. The clearest pattern in the Northern sky is the Big Dipper.

In the Southern sky, look out for the Cross, which you can see all year round.

You may be lucky enough to see a shooting star or satellites.

Airplanes have green lights on their starboard (right) wing and red lights on their port (left) wing.

The moon is big and easy to find. It takes about 28 days to circle the earth and we see different parts of it during that time.

Astronomers are scientists who study the sky. Modern astronomers use telescopes, computers, and even space shuttles to discover new things about the planets and space.

But *you too* can make a contribution to the science of astronomy. People who get to know the piece of sky above their home very well, sometimes discover new stars.

Wrap up well, take a notebook, a small flaslight and an adult with you, and off you go star-gazing!

Crystalized flowers

You can try different small flowers such as primroses, violets, daisies, and miniature roses or rose petals. Use to decorate small cakes.

What you will need
★ edible flowers
★ 1 egg white
★ 1 tsp water
★ fork, bowl, and saucer
★ 2 tbsp powdered sugar
★ small soft paintbrush
★ greaseproof paper
★ box with airtight lid

> **Warning!**
> These flowers are all edible but most are not. Don't eat anything unless you are absolutely sure it is safe!

1

Lightly beat the egg white and water until frothy. Put the sugar in a saucer.

2

Paint the flowers all over with the egg white mixture. Dip into sugar until completely covered.

3

Place on greaseproof paper and leave to dry overnight. Store carefully in an airtight box. They keep for about two weeks.

Spot the difference

Can you spot 10 differences between these two pictures?

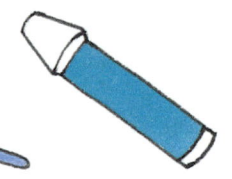

Making a kite

Kites originated in China and have been flown all over the world ever since. They have been used as weapons in wars, for rescuing shipwrecked sailors, as scarecrows over the Bali rice fields, to perform scientific experiments, and even with a line and hook to catch fish in Indonesia!

What you will need
- 2 lengths of thin wood dowelling, one of 22 in. and one 15 in.
- craft knife
- strong thread
- a large plastic bag (cut open)
- scissors
- sticky tape
- smaller plastic bags, different colors (cut open)
- ball of string

Warning!
Never put a plastic bag over your head. Cut along the sides and open before using.

1. Carefully cut notches into both ends of each piece of dowelling with the craft knife.

2. The short one should be 12 in. from the end of the long one.

Bind the sticks together at right angles with the thread.

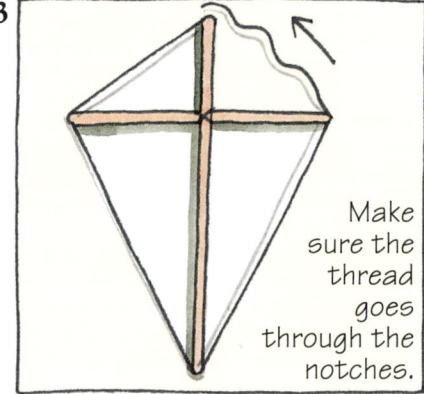

3. Make sure the thread goes through the notches.

Stretch some thread around the frame. Tie the ends at one of the notches.

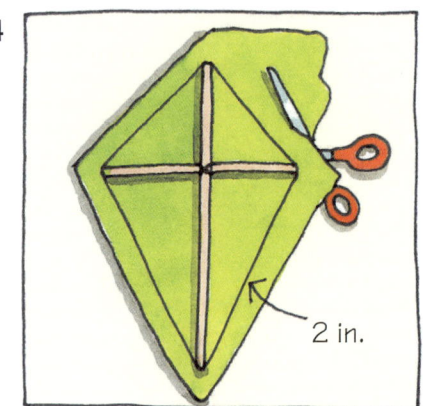

4. On a table, lay the frame on top of the plastic. Cut around the frame. Leave an extra 2 in. all around.

5. Cut the plastic around the notched ends as shown.

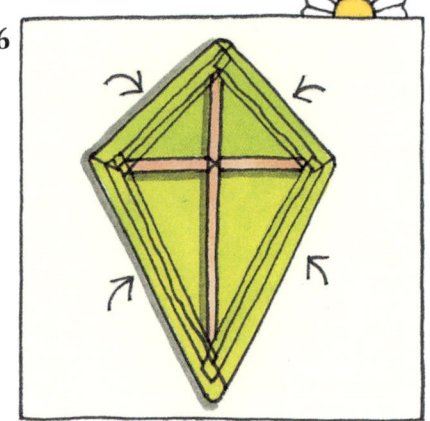

6. Fold the plastic around the thread and tape down.

7 Tie on to bottom of frame.

Make the tail. Cut colored plastic into strips and tie them along a 35.5 in. length of thread. Space them evenly.

8 Lastly, attach a piece of thread to form a loop 12 in. away from the front of the frame.

9 For your line, tie the end of a ball of string to the loop.

Make the tail a striking pattern of colors.

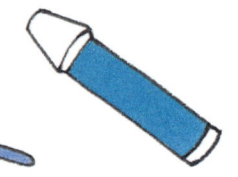

Painted pots

Plant these with annuals (flowers that grow for one year only).

What you will need
★ terracotta pots (wash old ones well)
★ waterproof paints, like acrylics or house gloss or matte paints
★ paintbrushes
★ masking tape

Warning! Make sure you protect your clothes with coveralls.

Floral—paint the outside of the pot in one color. When dry, paint simple flowers in two colors.

Stripy—tear masking tape and stick around the pot. Paint between. When dry, remove the tape.

Checked—paint stripes around the pot in one color. When dry, paint vertical stripes in contrasting colors.

Marbles

Marble games were played as far back as Egyptian and Roman times. Marbles were originally made from flint and stone and clay. Today most marbles are made of glass. They are different colors and sizes and very attractive.

For all the following games you need about 6 marbles per player.
shooter = the marble rolled

How to shoot
Knuckling down
Place the knuckle of your forefinger on the ground. Balance the marble in the bent forefinger. Put your thumb behind the marble and release it.

Flicking
Put the marble on the ground and flick it with your forefinger or middle finger.

Picking plums
For 2 or more players.
Draw a straight line on the ground in chalk or with a stick. Each player lays an equal number of marbles along the line, about 2 in. apart. Stand two metres away and take turns to roll a shooter at the line of marbles. If you hit one, you take it and have another go. You keep the marbles you hit and your shooter. If you don't hit a marble, you leave the shooter.

Continue until all the marbles have been won.

Bounce eye
For 2 or more players.
Mark a circle on the ground 12 in. in diameter. Each player puts one marble in the center.

Take it in turns to stand over the circle and drop a marble from eye height on to the marbles below.

You can keep any marbles you knock out of the circle plus your shooter.

If you don't knock a marble out, you leave your shooter in the circle.

Continue until the circle is empty.

Boss-out
For 2 players.
One player rolls a marble. When it stops, the second player tries to hit it with their shooter. If they hit it, they keep it. If not, the second player tries to hit the opponent's marble. When a marble is lost, the owner must retire, or produce another.

Daisy chain

Daisy chain
Make a crown or a necklace. Pick some daisies with nice long stems. Very carefully make a slit at the end of the stem with your fingernail. Push the stem of another daisy into the hole and pull it right through. Repeat until the chain is long enough. Then push the first daisy head through the last hole.

Four-leaved clover
The clover plant has three leaves. Very occasionally you find a four-leaved one. This is meant to bring you good luck. Press it to keep.

Braiding grasses
Pick three long grass stems and braid together. Make them into wristbands.

Dandelion clocks
You can "tell the time" by counting the number of puffs you need to blow away all the dandelion seeds on their small parachutes.

Playing games with grasses is a tradition in many countries of the world. Some Indigenous Australian children collected the seed heads of the rolling grass which grew on the sand dunes near the sea. They took them to the beach and tossed them into the air where they were blown along by the wind. Then they chased the seed heads and tried to pick them up while running at full speed. Ask older friends and relations if they know more games like this.

 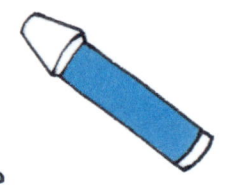

Getting ready to go

Vacations are exciting, but journeys can be boring when you have to sit for hours in the same seat.

Before you go, pack a travel bag with a few things that, with this book, will keep you busy on long car, train, boat, or plane journeys.

Packing list
★ lots of paper
★ pencils and sharpener
★ scissors
★ felt-tip pens
★ sticky tape
★ stick of glue
★ decorative stickers
★ photo corners
★ pack of cards

If possible, take a small tray to put on your knee for playing cards or coloring in.

Write names and addresses of friends and family on sticky labels, so you can send them postcards.

Decorate a shoe box to keep all your things in, or put them in your rucksack or bag. You won't need much room. Keep them handy wherever you are.

Most important of all—
DON'T FORGET THIS BOOK!

You can make a photo album or journal before you go. See pages 87 and 94.

You will need:
★ several big sheets of colored paper
★ a large blunt needle
★ yarn or string

If you feel travel sick don't read. Look out of the window, get plenty of fresh air if you can—breathe deeply.

On airplanes, sucking a candy during take-off and landing helps stop your ears "popping."

In the car, keep your seatbelt fastened!

Wear comfortable clothes and shoes.

 This compass will be hidden between pages 77 and 95. See if you can spot it.

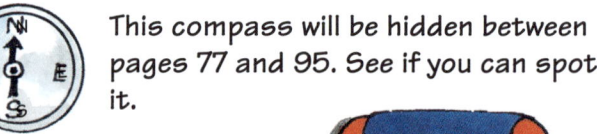

You can use the lid as a tray.

Nibbles and snacks

Prepare a few tasty snacks to enjoy on your journey. Avoid very sweet or salty things, as they'll make you thirsty. Try to avoid chocolatey, crumbly, and gooey foods too—they get everywhere.

Store everything in a plastic box or tin so it keeps fresh and doesn't get squashed.

Fruit

Fresh fruit such as grapes and apples should be washed and put in your box, with bananas.

Dried fruit is delicious—try raisins, apricots, figs, and dates, and the more unusual bananas and pineapple.

String the pieces into "necklaces" using a large blunt needle and thin string. Store the necklaces in your box, and nibble bits off when you feel like a snack.

Vegetables

Crunchy sticks of carrot and celery are great to munch on.

If you can get them, peas in their pods are delicious and sweet—and have their own packaging.

Take radishes and tiny tomatoes that you can pop into your mouth whole and are nice and juicy.

Nuts and seeds

These are very tasty and nutritious, but check with an adult first to make sure you're not allergic to nuts.

Add some paper napkins and a bottle of water to drink.

Finally—don't eat all your snacks at once right at the beginning of your journey, or you *will* get travel sick!

Spotting games

These games can be enjoyed while you are looking out of the window on a car or train journey. Remember not to distract the driver!

License plates

Work through the alphabet by spotting each letter at the beginning of license plates, in order.

Some countries show what town or state cars come from by their number plates. See how many you can spot.

You might see stickers on cars to show where they're from, too. Some of them are not easy—can you find out where they're all from?

Some number plates have three letters that form words, like "can" or "rot." See how many you can spot.

You can also make up silly phrases using the letters as the beginning of the words. For example, a number plate with the letters "SSD" could stand for "Stop Snoring Daddy!"

I spy

Take it in turns to spot something. If the outside is very boring you can spy inside. The "spy" says "I spy with my little eye something beginning with…" and gives the first letter of the word. The person who guesses correctly is the next "spy," and so on.

Black cat 10 points

For this game you need to write a list of objects and points in advance. The more unusual objects will score the highest points. For example, a swan could be 15 points, a black cat 10 points, a bakery 8 points, a fisherman 6 points, and a horse 2 points, and so on.

It's a good idea for players to look out of different sides of the car. You could end at a set time, or when someone gets a certain score.

Pencil and paper games

Make sure you have lots of paper and pencils and the time will fly by as you play these games.

Constantinople

See how many words you can make out of "Constantinople." The longest list wins. Try with other words—the name of the town or country you're going to, for example. You can add rules to make it harder, such as no proper names or slang words, and you can set a time limit.

Boxes

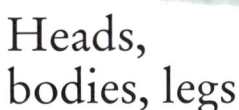

Draw 10 rows of 10 dots evenly on a piece of paper. Take it in turns to draw a line joining 2 dots. Each player tries to form boxes. If a player does make a box, they label it with their initial and draw an extra line. Carry on in turns. Be careful where you draw your line, especially as more boxes get finished—you don't want to make it easy for the others! The player with most boxes wins.

Heads, bodies, legs

Everyone has their own paper and pencil. First, draw a head at the top of the page—no peeking at the others! Then fold over your drawing, leaving only the neck lines showing. Now everyone passes their paper on to the next person. Then all draw a body attached to the neck lines and fold the paper over again so that just the tops of the legs are showing. Pass on again. Finish by drawing the legs and feet.

Now open the papers to find out what sort of monsters you've drawn!

Pick a letter

Each player has a pencil and paper. Take it in turns to think of a category—such as fruit, boys' names, animals, countries—and then a letter.

You all write down the most unusual thing you can think of beginning with that letter. At the end of the round you win a point if nobody else has thought of the same thing. The winner is the one with the most points.

Famous journeys

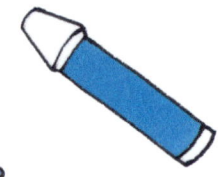

The Kon-Tiki expedition, 1947

No one knew where the people of the Polynesian islands, in the middle of the Pacific, originally came from. Norwegian explorer Thor Heyerdahl believed they were from Peru in South America, about 3,700 miles away.

To prove this, he and five companions built a raft using only what the ancient Peruvians would have used. They lashed balsa wood logs together with hemp rope, and made the two masts with mangrove wood.

The experts all thought it would sink, but the raft sailed well—helped along by the Humbold current and a strong easterly wind.

Food was no problem: flying fish landed on deck! But there were sharks too—the crew had a terrifying encounter with a gigantic whale shark. But they carried on valiantly.

After 102 days at sea the raft finally landed on one of the Polynesian islands. Thor Heyerdahl had proved that the voyage was possible.

Moonwalk, 1969

The most famous walk in history must be when the astronauts Neil Armstrong and Edwin Aldrin walked on the Moon.

On July 16 the Saturn V rocket carrying Apollo 11 launched from Cape Canaveral. When they had begun orbiting the Moon the two space men left their companion Michael Collins and crawled into the lunar module, nicknamed Eagle.

The Titanic's maiden voyage, 1912

The Titanic was the largest and most luxurious liner in the world. On April 10 she set off from Southampton to New York on her very first voyage. Crowds on the dock waved farewell.

The night of April 15 was freezing cold and moonless. The sea was flat calm. Suddenly one of the lookouts spotted an iceberg directly ahead. The ship began to turn but it was too late—the iceberg scraped the starboard bow. Metal plates buckled and rivets popped, letting huge volumes of water pour into the ship.

Now Captain Smith faced the worst. The ship everyone thought was UNSINKABLE was going down with 2,200 people on board and not enough lifeboats. It was a terrible struggle. The Titanic finally sank at 2:20am—2½ hours after the collision.

The tiny lifeboats drifted on an empty and freezing ocean with hundreds of people in the sea around them. The Carpathia, another liner, had received the Titanic's distress call and travelled at top speed to her rescue. 700 people were saved, but 1,500 perished. The survivors were taken to New York where friends and relatives waited. The tragedy shocked the world.

The world held its breath as Aldrin reported that their engine was blowing dust around on the surface of the Moon! Then came touchdown. Armstrong radioed to earth, "The Eagle has landed."

The two astronauts excitedly prepared for their historic walk. Armstrong was first. Placing his foot on the Moon he said, "That's one small step for man, one giant leap for mankind." He walked on the Moon for 2¼ hours, Aldrin slightly less. They collected over 44 lbs of rock and soil to take back for scientific investigation.

 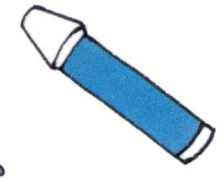

Card games

As long as you have a small flat surface within reach, you can play these card games.

Slap Jack

For two or three players
Place a shuffled pack of cards face down. Each player in turn takes a card and places it face up on a new pile. Whenever a Jack shows, all the players must clap hands overhead TWICE and then try to slap the Jack.

The player who first slaps the Jack takes all the "face up" cards. The game continues until all the Jacks have been taken.

The winner of the last Jack also takes any remaining "face down" cards. The person with the most cards wins.

War for two

For two players
Each player has 26 cards, face down in front of them. Together, each player turns over their top card on to a new pile. The one with the highest card takes them both and puts them face down at the bottom of his pile (King is high and Ace is low).

If the two cards have the same value, WAR breaks out: each player turns one card face down and a second face up. The one with the highest card takes all 6 cards.

If the second face up cards are also the same, the process is repeated, and this time the winner takes *all 10 cards!*

The game ends when one player has all the cards.

Old Maid

For three, four, or five players
Remove 3 Queens from the pack. The remaining Queen is the "Old Maid." Deal out all the cards.

First, each player looks at their cards and places any pairs face up in front of them. Then one player offers their hand (with the faces hidden) to the player on their left. This player takes one card, then puts down any pair it makes, as before. In turn, each player offers their hand to the person on their left, who takes a card.

The game continues until all the pairs are put down. The loser is the one left holding the Old Maid!

Word games

Some of these games are guessing games and others are a test of memory. In all cases, the sillier the items or words you choose, the more fun you will have.

What am I?

One person thinks of a creature and the others try and guess what it is by asking questions like "Do you have fur?," "Do you eat meat?". You may only answer yes or no. The winning "guesser" goes next.

To vary the game, agree to be a piece of furniture, an item of clothing, a fruit, and so on.

Packing

One person starts by thinking of something beginning with the letter "a," then says, "I'm packing a suitcase and I put in... an *a*pricot," for example. The next person thinks of something beginning with "b" and adds it on: "I'm packing a suitcase and put in an *a*pricot and a *b*alloon." Each person adds something to the list starting with the next letter of the alphabet. As the list gets longer it gets harder to remember everything—see how far you can get!

Alphabet food

Take it in turns to name foods beginning with each letter of the alphabet, in order. Example: Apple, bun, cookies, doughnut, egg, and so on until… Z!

You can play this game with animals or drinks instead—or you could think of your own categories.

Place chain

One player says a place name and the next player must think of another place beginning with the last letter of that name. So: London might lead to New Orleans, which in turn might lead to St. Louis. The places can be in any country, but you mustn't repeat any of them. If someone can't think of a name, they stop playing.

Exercises

Sitting still for a long time can be very boring. Here are some simple exercises you can do in your seat to make you feel more comfortable. Take off your shoes first.

Remember, keep your seatbelt fastened if you're in a car!

Arms stretch
Clasp hands together and slowly raise arms up and back until they are over your head. Now stretch as high as you can and turn palms upwards. Slowly lower arms and relax. Repeat 4 times.

Knees bend
Clasp hands together and pull right knee up close to chest. Hold for a count of 8. Lower leg. Repeat with left knee and then with both knees together. Repeat 4 times.

Feet
Stretch right foot from the ankle. Bend toes forwards and back. Slowly move foot in a circle clockwise, then the other way. Repeat with the left foot.

Hands
Stretch left hand forward from wrist. Bend fingers up and down. Slowly move hand in a circle clockwise, then the other way. Repeat with right hand.

Head and neck
Sit well back in seat. Turn head to the right and slowly raise and lower chin 3 times. Repeat with head turned to the left. Repeat 4 times.

Deep breathing
Now relax completely. Sit back in your seat. Close your eyes and take a deep breath, hold for a little while then slowly let your breath out. Repeat 4 times.

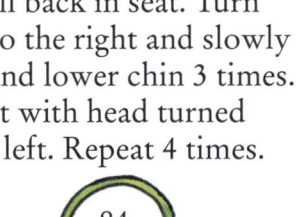

Odd bag out

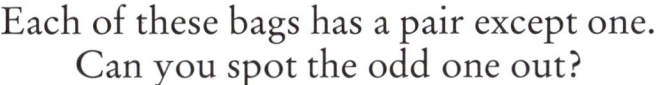

Each of these bags has a pair except one.
Can you spot the odd one out?

Happy snaps

Make a photographic record of your vacation—it's the best kind of souvenir.

Put a film in your camera before you set off, so you can take a photo as soon as you like.

Keep the strap around your neck and hold the camera still when taking a photo.

Tips on taking photographs

Try and remember to take photographs all through your vacation. Don't leave it until the last couple of days—it might be raining!

Take photos of where you are staying, of your favorite café, and so on, as well as the more obvious ones of your family.

When you take a picture, don't stand too far back. Get people as large as you can in the frame, but don't cut off their heads or feet! Before you press the button check that everything is in the frame, and isn't crooked.

Why not take a photo of the new friends you have met on vacation? If you swap addresses, you could send them a copy.

Get someone to take a photo of ALL of you at least once on vacation.

Don't take pictures of people standing in front of a window or bright light, as their faces will be dark. Light should preferably fall on your subject from one side.

Look out for good postcards instead of taking lots of photos of the landscape.

Look for some more unusual subjects, like windows, signposts, or numbers, or things in your favorite color. Whenever you're away, look for the same thing and build up a collection.

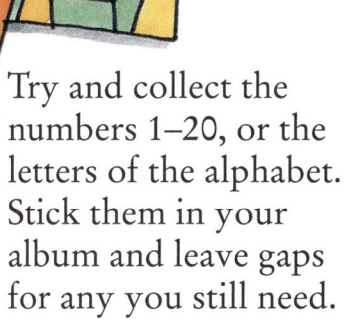

Try and collect the numbers 1–20, or the letters of the alphabet. Stick them in your album and leave gaps for any you still need.

Make a thank you card for someone you stayed with or visited. Stick one of your photos on colored paper and draw a border around it.

Photo album

You can easily make your own album before you go, or while you're away. Fold about three large sheets of colored paper in half, then stitch them together along the fold with yarn, using a large blunt needle.

Darker colors will show up your photos best. The pages don't have to be the same color.

You could cut the place name out of a brochure and stick it on your album cover with the vacation dates.

Use glue or photo corners.

Plan the page before you glue anything. Remember to leave room to write the date, who or what the picture is of, and where you took it. Do it soon—it's easy to forget!

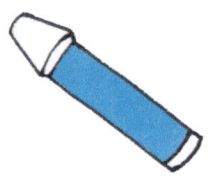

Spot the difference

Can you spot 10 differences between these two pictures?

Finger puppets

These finger puppets are made from paper, with holes for your fingers. Keep the shapes very simple. Decorate them with pens and sticky shapes.

Draw a head and body on to paper—your fingers will be the legs. Cut out your figure.

Near the bottom, draw around a coin for the leg holes. Push closed scissors through the center of each ring and then cut out neat holes.

Think of plays you could put on with dancers, animals, clowns, acrobats—whoever you want to make!

Cut a hole in the center for the elephant's trunk.

Draw your favorite soccer players in their strip and have a game using a piece of crumpled paper as a ball. Use a paper cup on its side as the goal.

Rainbow patterns

Color these patterns, starting in the center and working your way out to the edges.

Think about your colors before you start. Will you use warm colors—oranges, reds, and pinks, or cool colors: blues, greens, and mauves?

Try drawing your own pattern. Start at the center and work outwards.

You could stage a competition to see who can produce a design that makes your eyes zing!

Songs and games

Sing-songs are great fun, but perhaps not for others sitting near you on a plane or train—so keep singing for the privacy of car journeys!

Here are some good songs for travelling:

- Row, Row, Row Your Boat
- Runaway Train
- Wheels on the Bus
- Bicycle built for two

Can you think of any more about cars, boats, planes, trains, or bicycles?

You can adapt songs everyone knows, too: for example, use silly suggestions for animals in *Old MacDonald had a farm*, like "on that farm he had two dinosaurs!"

Guess the tune

Clap in time to a tune in your head and ask a friend to try and guess what it is. Keep it simple.

Hokey cokey

Try a version of this old favorite but put *small* bits of your body in and out—like your nose, ear, or toe. Can you think of any other silly parts to shake about?

Simon says

Here's another favorite that you can adapt for sitting down. Each player in turn gives the command "Simon says…"—bounce up and down, wriggle your knees, clap your hands, shake your head, and so on.

Remember that if the caller doesn't say "Simon says," you mustn't obey the command! The quicker you give the commands, the more fun it is.

Knees, hands, fingers

This action and spelling game starts slowly and then speeds up as everyone gets the hang of it. Keep going even if someone doesn't think of a word quickly enough.

All together, first clap hands on knees, then clap hands, then snap fingers. On the finger-snapping, the first person says a letter of the alphabet. On the next snap, the next person has to say a word beginning with that letter. Keep going, alternating letters and words.

Hand jive

Hand jiving was popular years ago at rock and roll concerts, when audiences "danced" in their seats using hand movements, whole rows together. See if you can make up a sequence to the tune and words of a favorite song. Some movements you could use are clapping, pointing, waving, thumbs up, knocking fists together, holding elbows, and so on.

Move both hands together and keep in time with a friend.

Paper, scissors, stone

For two players
With one hand, both players knock three times and on the count of four hold out a hand in one of the positions below: scissors, paper or stone. The "strongest" one wins: scissors can cut paper, stone can blunt scissors, and paper can wrap stone. If both players do the same thing it's a tie, so try again. The winner is the best of five turns.

Singing rounds

You can choose a round that everyone knows, or teach each other new ones. Does anyone know *Three blind mice* or *Frère Jacques*? Practise together first. When you're ready, one person starts off alone. After the first phrase the next person starts the song too, and so on. Carry on until everyone has joined in, if you can.

When you get to the end of the song you just start again from the beginning—if laughing and a sore throat haven't stopped you already!

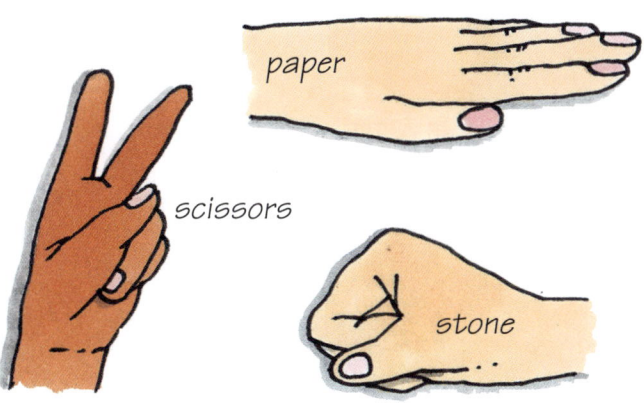

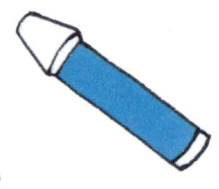

Travel journal

A wonderful reminder of your vacation is a diary illustrated with bits and pieces you have collected on your trip.

You can take a scrapbook away with you and write a little about each day as you go along. Stick in tickets, postcards, and interesting things you find. Or you can collect and keep things until you get home and do it then. If you want to leave it until the end of your vacation, make a few notes of what you do and see each day while you are away so you don't miss out important details later.

foreign coins

tickets

postcards

You can also ask friends and family for the postcards you sent them, if they'll give them back! Then you'll also have the stamps and the postmarks showing where you sent them from, and when.

candy wrappers

brochures

Keep everything flat and safe until you need it—perhaps slip it into a book or magazine.

restaurant bills

drink coasters

empty matchboxes

sugar cubes or packets

Long after your vacation is over you'll have something to remind you of it—and a lovely record to show others.

You can make your own book or album—see page 87. Look at what you've collected before you start sticking anything down. You might want to arrange pages according to different subjects, such as "eating" or "days out"—or you could take the vacation day by day. Start with setting off.

Glue carefully on the back of items. Try to avoid sticky tape—it doesn't last.

Pressed wild flowers or leaves are unusual additions. Only pick one good specimen, however, and *never* pick rare flowers or plants! If you're not sure, ask an adult.

You can include your photos in the journal, or ask adults for some of theirs. But don't use too many—this is not a photo album.

To press them, place your flowers between some tissue in a book, or under something heavy. Then put them in a small clear plastic bag or some cellophane, and glue them into your book.

Try some sketching while you're away!

Ask people you meet and make friends with on vacation for their autographs.

A friendly waiter or waitress might be willing to autograph the bill.

Answers

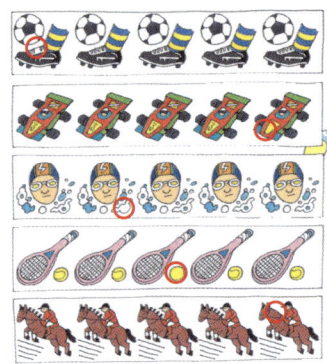
page 23

page 85

page 16

page 64

page 36

page 69

page 88

© b small publishing 2019
Originally published as Turn off the TV, Best Friends, Fresh Air Fun, and Are We There Yet? Activity Books
First Racehorse for Young Readers Edition 2019.
All rights to any and all materials in copyright owned by the publisher are strictly reserved by the publisher.
Racehorse for Young Readers books may be purchased in bulk at special discounts for sales promotion, corporate gifts, fund-raising, or educational purposes. Special editions can also be created to specifications. For details, contact the Special Sales Department, Racehorse for Young Readers, 307 West 36th Street, 11th Floor, New York, NY 10018 or info@skyhorsepublishing.com.
Racehorse for Young Readers ™ is a pending trademark of Skyhorse Publishing, Inc.®, a Delaware corporation.
Visit our website at www.skyhorsepublishing.com.
10 9 8 7 6 5 4 3 2 1
Library of Congress Cataloging-in-Publication Data is available on file.
Design: Louise Millar
Editorial: Catherine Bruzzone and Sam Hutchinson
Production: Madeleine Ehm
Cover design by Louise Millar
Cover artwork by Clare Beaton
Print ISBN: 978-1-63158-455-8
Ebook ISBN: 978-1-63158-457-2
Printed in China